Latina DIY Skincare
Make Facial Products from Home Like a Pro.
Catalina Charpentier B.

ISBN: 978-1-961176-12-6 (eBook)

ISBN: 978-1-961176-13-3 (Paperback)

ISBN: 978-1-961176-14-0 (Hardback)

Publisher: ARTEMIX BEAUTY, Owasso, Oklahoma

Website: www.artemixbeauty.com

Instagram: @artemixbeauty

Facebook: @artemixbeauty

JUST FOR YOU

NATURAL EXTRACTS TO ENHANCE YOUR COSMETICS

Basic DIY Anti-Aging Secrets using Plant-Based Ingredients

CATALIANA CHARPENTIER B.

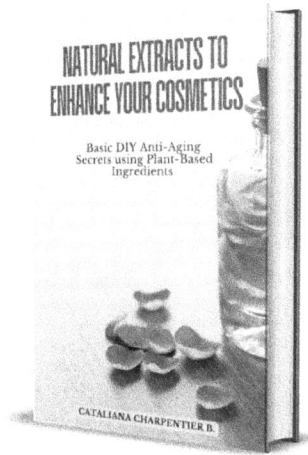

A FREE GIVEAWAY

Learn about Natural Anti-Aging Extracts

WWW.ARTEMIXBEAUTY.COM

www.artemixbeauty.com

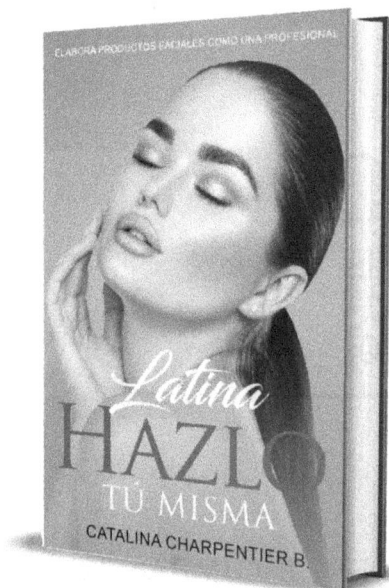

ELABORA PRODUCTOS FACIALES COMO UNA PROFESIONAL

Latina
HAZLO
TÚ MISMA

CATALINA CHARPENTIER B.

¡Lleva tu cuidado de la piel al siguiente nivel! Descubre cómo crear productos naturales como un profesional desde la comodidad de tu hogar.

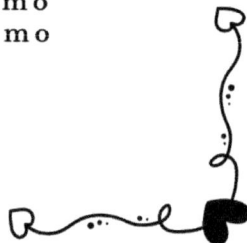

Contents

Introduction   1

1. The Skin and Its pH   9
   Understanding Skin Types
   Tips to Maintain Skin pH

2. Work Center and Supplies   23
   Understanding Cosmetic Ingredients
   Setting up Your Workstation
   Ingredients Needed for a Cosmetics Lab
   Understanding the Solubility of Ingredients

3. Principles of Cosmetic Chemistry   45
   Understanding Cosmetic Components
   The Function of Ingredients
   Deciphering Cosmetic Labeling Requirements

4. Manufacture of Basic Products   57
   Permitted Cosmetic Preservatives
   Mixing Cosmetic Preservative
   Preparing Base Materials
   Creating Base Creams
   Cosmetic Gel Base
   Soap Base

5. Products for Stained Faces   85

Depigmenting Cream

Depigmenting Cream From Scratch

Depigmenting Toner

Depigmenting Vitamin C Serum

Moisturizing Protective Day Cream

Useful Acids in Cosmetic Products

6. Products for Oily Skin   99

Moisturizing Daytime Gel for Oily Skin

Revitalizing Serum for Oily Skin

Cleansing Gel for Oily Skin

Dermoprotective Facial Soap

7. Anti-Aging Products   109

Biphasic Makeup Remover

Cleansing Milk

Nourishing Anti-Wrinkle Repair Cream

8. Products for Sensitive Skin   115

Cleansing Foam

Moisturizer for Sensitive Skin

Soothing Toner for Sensitive Skin

9. Products for Dark Circles   121

Eye Contour Cream

Eye Contour Gel Cream

Strengthening Serum for Lashes and Brows

10. Complementary Products   131

Nourishing Lip Balm

Preservative-Free Raspberry Lip Balm

Facial Scrub

Serum for All Skin Types

11. Conclusion   139

12. Glossary   147

13. References   153

Introduction

One of the particularities of a culture inherited from our ancestors is natural medicine. Latinos like to create home remedies, concoctions, and natural methods to solve health problems and care for our skin. The women of our culture have an innate curiosity to create, protect, and heal, so this book will help us to enjoy creating formulas that benefit us while nourishing our skin with the help of nature. We know all too well that using the wrong products can turn our skin dry, dull, and flaky. Worse still, acne and blemishes can result from improper care. What is a woman to do? We try the methods beauty bloggers rave about and live with the knowledge that our cosmetic reactions might grow mold and turn rancid. Such waste seems to be an inescapable consequence of going the homemade route, but this does not have to be the case. Creating effective, safe, and stable cosmetics at home can easily be done! All you need is an understanding of the basic principles of formulation and the characteristics that make Latina skin unique.

Latina skin is wonderfully diverse, ranging from sumptuous mocha, to sultry bronzes and subtle honey (and all the gorgeous shades in between). Thanks to our unique skin, we tan easily and develop wrinkles much later than our fair-skinned counterparts, but the extra melanin does have a drawback: Stains develop easier.

Many products on the market are formulated generically to appeal to as large an audience as possible. There is nothing inherently wrong with that, but these generic formulations do not take the special characteristics or problems that Latin skin faces into consideration. Dark circles, adult acne, melasma, and other blemishes make it challenging to give our skin the love and care it deserves, especially when relying on mass-produced products. Beauty costs, but the sad truth is that there is no guarantee those exclusive brand names we love splurging on will deliver the best possible care for our skin. Creating cosmetic products is a surprisingly simple and satisfying process, plus, the formulations covered in this book are developed specifically to satisfy the needs of Latina skin, leaving it soft and radiant. Other than giving the skin optimal care, there are other benefits when formulating your own cosmetics at home. These include:

- Controlling the quality of raw material. What you put in is what you get out! This is true for skincare and cosmetic products alike. By taking charge of the manufacturing process and opting for the best quality we can find, we are guaranteed to create skincare products that will deliver far superior results. Every Latina and her *abuela* will be asking what your skincare secret is!

- Detoxifying the skin with natural, pure ingredients. Cosmetic products can contain unnecessary and sometimes harmful ingredients. By removing redundant ingredients from the formulation, we maximize the nourishing properties of these products without introducing ingredients that may irritate or harm the skin.

- Avoiding mass-produced items that are chemical-laden and expensive. Just because that age-defying serum cost upwards of $12 0.00 does not mean it will deliver the results promised! More often than not, the ingredients list on well-loved brands include fillers and other hard-to-pronounce chemicals that no self-respecting skincare professional would recommend! So why should we treat our faces like a toxic dump when there are better and more effective alternatives?

More importantly, when we create cosmetic products at home, we are guaranteed that the product is fresh. This means the active ingredients used will have a more significant and dramatic effect on the skin. As a skincare professional, the number one reason I'd encourage women to create their own cosmetics is this: Wrinkles are also produced by the accumulation of chemicals that do not allow the skin to breathe. By creating our own skincare products, we are eliminating those chemicals that suffocate the skin, giving us youthful, radiant skin well into our older years. It is a win-win all round! The formulations in this book suggest a maximum dosage of the active ingredients without compromising the product's stability, making them more effective in skincare.

Those who enjoy creating cosmetics will find a lot of value tucked away in this book. You'll become familiar with basic cosmetic principles, formulations, and much more—useful information for hobbyists and entrepreneurs alike. This information contained in this book, in addition to helping entrepreneurs discover alternative solutions to skincare problems that plague Latina women, can help them start a lucrative business in their community. Information is power, and self-empowerment is the most powerful form of emancipation available in our modern world. In short, Latinas should own their beauty and take charge of their skincare.

Cosmetic products created by Latinas for Latin skin should be the norm. Before we get ahead of ourselves, though, there are some important things we need to keep in mind when embarking on this journey. To get the best out of your cosmetic creations and to avoid wastage, it is important to keep the following points in mind.

- **Use the right formula**

Different cosmetic products have different formulations. When developing cosmetic creations, it is important to use formulations that remain stable and nourishes the skin. We should consider our ingredients and how they interact with each other when creating cosmetics.

- **Make use of a preservative system**

Most cosmetics have preservatives, and for good reason. These ingredients help to keep the product stable and safe to use. Water-based products and some anhydrous formulations need preservatives to safeguard them against yeast, mold, and bacteria. A good rule of thumb to follow is this: If there's water in the cosmetic formulation, add a preservative. You'll learn all about preservatives in chapter four, so I won't dive too deep here.

Entrepreneurs wanting to bring life to a cosmetic creation will need to test their product's stability, along with microbiological tests. This helps to determine a fairly accurate expiration date if the preservatives work as they should. Don't worry, these tests are quite simple and are of great help when taking your product to market. Using quality ingredients is the secret to maximizing shelf life. For oil-based products, it is best to protect them against oxidation by adding vitamin E (or another suitable antioxidant) to the formulation.

- **Store products correctly**

Choosing gorgeous packaging is great fun, but the container needs to keep cosmetic creations safe and stable. DIY cosmetics need to be stored in hygienic containers at all times. Wherever possible, use a pump, spray valve, drop dispenser, or spatula with cosmetic products to limit contamination.

- **Keep batches small**

It is difficult to know the exact expiration date of DIY cosmetics. This increases the risk of product spoilage quite a bit. To limit wastage, it is prudent to produce cosmetics in small batches. This ensures the cream, gel, preservative, or extracts that you are using are as fresh as possible. When whipping up anhydrous products, always ensure to package them suitably and remember to add an antioxidant. Unpreserved water-based products should only be made in single doses when needed. That's because microbes love water-based products and easily grow in these formulations. Limiting these products to single uses when needed is one of the safest ways to use these products.

- **Measure ingredients carefully**

Ingredients need to be measured carefully to achieve consistent results. Use a digital scale to measure liquids and solids accurately each time. If you are adjusting a formulation or trying something new, write down the process and recipe. That way you'll be able to replicate if the end product is a desirable one, but this advanced step is only recommended once you have mastered the basics. In this book, the formulations are shared with the optimal ingredient amounts to obtain excellent results, not only in the integrity of the product but also in the results obtained with use. Building a skincare brand rests heavily on the quality of the products we create.

- **Respect ingredients**

Knowing what is in our cosmetic products is a big motivator that inspires many to create their own products. It is a wonderfully creative outlet, but we need to understand and respect how ingredients are used in a formulation. This is a topic we'll cover in Chapters 2 and 3. Don't worry, when you master the basics, creating quality cosmetic products becomes surprisingly easy! Many cosmetic ingredients come with usage instructions, and it is highly recommended to follow these. Many ingredients can lead to skin irritation and reactions if used and prepared incorrectly.

- **Adjust pH**

This simple step is vital to keep DIY cosmetics stable and safe for as long as possible. The pH of a product impacts different characteristics of the formulation. For example, the preservative may not function properly or the look, feel and scent of the product is different from what you expected. Simple pH strips and a few minutes of quality checking can save you from a lot of potential product spoilage. We'll delve a bit deeper into this topic a bit later in the book.

- **Observe proper production practices**

A key issue when creating cosmetic products is to avoid contamination at all stages. Choosing the right preservative is important, but so is the production process. We need to work clean and never use our cosmetic production tools for anything else. This is to limit contamination, maximizing the quality and shelf life of the end product. Don't worry! The principles of cosmetic chemistry are surprisingly easy to grasp and are covered in the book.

This book will give you insight into the practices, ingredients, and equipment needed to safely formulate quality DIY cosmetic products. Observing the above-mentioned practices will help to keep the quality of our products high waist, minimizing spoilage. The simple steps and detailed insights are designed to help you express your cosmetic creations as safe, effective, and quality products. Creating cosmetics can be an exciting journey, one that I am eager to share with you.

Keep in mind that to obtain good health and figure, we must feed ourselves with fresh and unprocessed food and avoid items that are frozen or preserved with cheap chemicals (like those mass-produced garage pies). Our skin works the same way. It is not convenient to bombard it with mass-produced chemicals because, sooner or later, this accumulates in our skin and body. As a result, we will show what we have consumed for years. For this reason, making your products guarantees you to fully understand the components with which you are feeding your skin and how fresh food will give your face a new look as well, but above all, it is naturally healthy! And that is the most important part. So journey with me as we discover easy products to make at home for fabulously flawless skin.

·❤ · ❤ · ❤ · ❤ · ❤ ·

1

The Skin and Its pH

Our skin is incredible at multitasking. It performs many essential roles that contribute to our overall well-being. The skin works as a protective barrier, protecting us from diseases, injuries, and extreme temperatures. One of the protection mechanisms that the skin employs is pH. The skin is constantly exposed to external aggressions, so maintaining its optimal pH is essential to the skin's fundamental role of protection. When the pH of our skin becomes compromised a whole range of problems can surface ranging from infection, rosacea, and atopic dermatitis (*Understanding Skin–Skin's PH*, 2017).

The acid mantle helps to keep our skin healthy. It is a thin layer of lipids and amino acids that plays a key role in the skin's protective barrier. Our acid mantle helps to inhibit the growth of bacteria and neutralizes alkaline-based aggressors (harsh surfactants being one of them). This is important to maintain an optimal environment to allow the natural flora on our skin to thrive.

When our skin's pH creeps into the alkaline range, this natural balance becomes disturbed. In an alkaline environment, important epidermal lipids can't be synthesized, causing the skin to lose water and dry out, compromising the outer layer of the skin and its protective function. This can lead to the skin becoming more sensitive to environmental triggers, leaving us with dry, sensitive skin that is susceptible to infection and disease. So maintaining the proper pH of our skin is a pretty big deal!

The pH of our skin varies a tiny bit with age, gender, and the area of the body (armpits, genitals, and hands have a slightly different pH than the rest of the body). To measure the pH of the skin and many other substances, we make use of the pH scale. The scale's values range from 0 to 14. A pH of 7 is considered neutral. Any value below this would be deemed acidic, and any value higher than 7 is alkaline. Our skin's natural pH is a touch on the acidic side, running between 4.5 and 5.9 on the pH scale. The optimal pH value for skin care products is widely agreed to be 5.5. Different skin types also have different pH levels. The pH for each skin type is indicated as follows:

- Oily skin: Between 4.9 and 5.0

- Normal skin: Between 5.2 and 5.5

- Dry skin: Between 5.7 and 5.9

Skin types are directly related to the amount of sweat and sebaceous secretions that forms on the surface layer of the face. Optimum secretion means that your skin surface is well-lubricated and moisturized, i.e. normal skin. Alterations of these secretions give rise to different skin types. We'll examine different skin types a little later.

External factors can stress the skin and impact the pH. These factors range from changes in humidity and temperature, pollution and dirt, cleansing the skin too much, and using alkaline cosmetics and products and chemicals. Chemicals with an alkaline pH can be particularly detrimental to our skin. These chemicals damage the skin's protective barrier by overtaxing our skin's natural ability to neutralize alkalis. One such chemical is Sodium Lauryl Sulfate (SLS). This surfactant is commonly used in shampoos and body washes because it foams easily and is cheap. Most of us associate that foaminess with cleanliness, not realizing that SLS strips the skin of its natural oils, leaving it dry and vulnerable to environmental aggressors. Research confirms that SLS is a known irritant and can lead to a myriad of problems including skin and eye irritations, dermatitis, eczema, psoriasis, skin rashes, hormonal disruptions, and the odd dizzy spell and headache (Geier et al., 2003).

Internal factors (genetics, hormones, and biological age) also affect our skin's pH. Keep in mind that our protective acid mantle takes time to form, this is why newborn babies have incredibly sensitive skin. Fortunately, there are ways we can support the skin's optimum pH level. Healthy lifestyle choices and a regular skincare routine with products that respect your skin's pH goes a long way to reduce and prevent problems.

· ♥ · ♥ · ♥ · ♥ · ♥ ·

Understanding Skin Types

Internal factors (age, genetics, hormones) and external factors (pollution, temperature, alkaline cosmetics, chemicals) affect our skin and cause its pH to be destabilized. In dry skin, the lipid protection barrier is shallow. This causes an increased risk of dryness, tenderness, and dehydration. When these conditions occur and the skin becomes sensitized, the pH changes and becomes more acidic than the average oily skin (which has a pH between 4.9 and 5.0). The impact on our skin can be quite devastating, leading the sebaceous gland to atrophy due to excess fat on the skin's surface. This results in an imbalance of the skin's pH, and in some cases, can push the skin's pH level close to neutral (7 on the pH scale).

When it comes to the different tones of Latino skin, the number of melanocytes in our skin can complicate things considerably. Melanocytes produce melanin. This is what gives our skin those gorgeous sultry tones, but too much melanin production can lead to dark spots and stains. Add to this that we are more likely to develop visible dark circles or develop acne-prone skin when the skin is oily, and skincare becomes a whole new ballgame. No wonder Latinas spent well over two billion dollars on cosmetic products in 2021 (Burhop Fallon, 2021)! Keeping those wrinkles at bay is a pricey exercise, especially when relying on products that don't consider the uniqueness of your skin.

In this context, there are classifications and subclassifications that dermatologists and dermocosmeatras study in more depth. You may have noticed that cosmetic products are always formulated to serve a specific skin type. Different skin types have different needs and their products are formulated to satisfy the skin's specific needs. This is why we won't use products formulated for dry skin on oily or combination skin, for example. Products designed for dry skin types tend to have strong emollient and hydration properties, which may lead to a greasy appearance and clogged pores when used on oily or combination skin. Each skin type needs a different approach to care with dedicated products. To unveil the mystery surrounding skin types, we'll take a closer look at normal, oily, dry, combination, and sensitive skin types.

Normal Skin

This skin type has a pH of 5.5 to 5.7 and is in balance with regard to sebaceous secretions and sweat production. The skin is soft and uniform, with a slight shine and barely visible pores. It is very typical to find this skin type in younger people and children. This skin type tends to be low-maintenance, but can become dry when neglected. Despite having optimal conditions, normal skin needs proper care to be protected from external agents and to prevent any disruptions to its secretory balance. As time passes, normal skin may become dry or oily. The best way to take care of this is to identify which direction the skin is heading (dry or oily) and then alternate the use of creams and gels according to how the skin is responding. Normal skin should be cleansed twice daily, in the morning when we wake up and in the evening before going to bed. Cleansing should be done before hydrating and nourishing the skin.

Dry Skin

This skin type has a pH of 5.9 to 6.1. This skin type is characterized by being very thin with minimal elasticity. It is also reactive to external stimuli and has a tendency to show dilations of small blood vessels near the surface of the skin. If you notice that your skin has these characteristics along with it being dull and prone to wrinkles and flaking, you've likely got dry skin and will need to treat it with extra love. Dry skin types are quite sensitive to climate changes and can have a dull appearance and rough feel. Good hydration is key to treating dry skin.

Dry skin needs to be washed twice a day and hydrated immediately with the appropriate amount of cream. At night, it is best to use a revitalizing cream with greater unctuousness (oiliness). This will help to nourish the skin and give the active ingredients time to work their magic. Dry skin can usually be found in adults over 35 years of age (mature skin) and in individuals who have a tendency towards dry skin.

Dehydrated Skin

Dehydrated skin is often confused with dry skin, but the two are not the same. Dry skin is characterized by a lack of lipids, which is why the use of oil-containing products is encouraged. Dehydrated skin is recognized by its lack of water. Dry and oily skin types can develop this variant and the main symptom is a deep feeling of tightness and flaking in the middle area of the face, edges of the nose, and the eyebrow. To address dehydrated skin, we need to use products that provide water. The day and night creams should be supported with a decongestant moisture toner formulated for dry skin. In the case of dehydrated oily skin, gels and tones should be used as needed.

Some lifestyle changes are necessary to successfully treat dehydrated skin. We can conduct a simple test to find out if the skin is dehydrated or not. All you need to do is lightly pinch the skin around the cheek area. Watch the pinched area closely. Do you notice wrinkling? If so, let the pinched portion go. Does the skin bounce back immediately? If not, chances are you've got dehydrated skin. A skincare professional can help you to classify your skin type if you are unsure.

Oily Skin

If your skin is oily, it likely has a pH between 4.9 and 5.1. Oily skin tends to have a thick texture, enlarged pores, and is moist to the touch. Individuals with this skin type typically have a shiny appearance all over their face. One of the biggest challenges that come with oily skin is to keep blackheads and pimples under control, as pores can vlog easily. The upside of having oily skin is that we tend to see fewer wrinkles, but the drawback is that the risk of developing pimples increases. This skin is quite resistant to external agents, so it is not recommended to use any oil derivative (such as cream). Regular exfoliation is important to keep the skin smooth and free from dirt. Oily skin can be caused by a variety of factors like hormonal imbalance, genetics, climate, age, lifestyle, and diet. The best way to turn things around for this skin type is to get to the root of the problem and follow an appropriate skincare plan.

Individuals with oily skin should cleanse their face twice daily and use hydrating gels that quickly absorb into the skin. These gels are water-based, which is helpful for fat control. At night, it is best to use a revitalizing gel or serum. In Chapter 4 of this book, you'll learn how to make fast-absorbing, skin-loving gels that will nourish your skin without that unpleasant sticky sensation some products leave on your skin.

Combination Skin

This skin type is also known as mixed skin and can be a challenge to manage. The reason for this is that these skin types combine characteristics of normal and oily skin. Managing combination skin involves addressing opposite problems in the same area of the face, such as dryness and oiliness. Mixed skin types typically exhibit an oily nose, forehead, and chin (the T-zone), while the cheeks are dry. A weekly exfoliation and nourishing mask are recommended to help bring out the best in these skin types. There are a number of factors that can lead to combination skin, but most of the time it comes down to a roll of the genetic dice. Seasonal changes and incorrect skincare products often exacerbate the problem, encouraging excessive sebum production in the T-zone while drying the cheeks out. When formulating for mixed skin types, it is best to avoid the following ingredients:

- Alcohol, denatured alcohol, and witch hazel–common ingredients in toners.

- Highly abrasive scrubs.

- Using strong fragrances in the product. Fragrance is a common culprit behind many instances of skin irritation, regardless if the ingredient is synthetic or natural in origin.

Sensitive Skin

A highly reactive skin type, sensitive skin will react to stimuli that won't bother normal skin types. You may fall into this category if your skin is constantly irritated. This is often accompanied by burning, itching, and redness due to climatic factors. To care for this skin variant, we should avoid products that contain fragrances and high concentrations of preservatives. For this reason, products geared toward sensitive skin care usually omit the usage of fragrances and colorants. The more natural the skincare, the better. Inappropriate cosmetic products, alcohol consumption, emotional conditions, and hormones can act as triggers that irritate sensitive skin. The reaction usually goes hand in hand with discomfort, tightness, redness, or itching. That's because the protective function of the skin is compromised and will need a greater degree of gentle care. In the sensitive skin category, we will find photosensitive and hypersensitive skin types.

- **Photosensitive skin:** Photosensitivity is often referred to as a "sun allergy," an apt, but slightly simplistic explanation. Photosensitivity is a condition where the skin becomes highly sensitive to ultraviolet light (*Photosensitivity*, 2011). It does not matter if the UV rays come from the sun or from a tanning bed, the result is the same: Skin that burns easily. The skin may become painful and itchy following exposure to UV rays, and in some cases, will blister and peel. Photosensitivity can be caused by certain medications, such as anticancer drugs, and medical conditions, like lupus and xeroderma. To treat photosensitive skin, it is advised to consult a skincare professional.

- **Hypersensitive skin:** Very sensitive skin is an unpleasant and common condition characterized by dry skin, irritation, pimples, eczema, redness, as well as burning and stinging sensations (*Hypersensitivity in General*, n.d.). As you probably guessed, this skin type is the result of a compromised skin barrier and will need special care. Lifestyle changes may be necessary to treat this condition, as certain fabrics and dyes can irritate this skin type.

• ❤ • ❤ • ❤ • ❤ • ❤ •

Tips to Maintain Skin pH

The pH of our skin plays an incredibly important role in maintaining its overall health. Don't worry, maintaining the pH balance is easier than you think. Keep in mind that after cleansing the face, it normally takes an hour or two for the skin to return to its normal pH level (Debayle, 2018). During this time, the acid mantle is vulnerable, and the skin needs to be treated with extra care. With that in mind, let's take a look at some proactive steps we can take to protect our skin.

- **Avoid over cleansing:** When we over-cleanse the skin, we strip away the protective barrier and this leads to dryness and irritation. Ideally, we should cleanse the skin twice a day (morning and night) with a gentle cleanser that is suited for your skin type. A gentle cleanser will not contain any Sodium Lauryl Sulfate (SLS) or abrasive elements. Rinse the skin with lukewarm water or use micellar water to remove any excess oil after a bath.

- **Avoid extreme exfoliation:** Exfoliation is good for the skin. It helps to remove dead skin cells from the surface of our skin, but we should be careful about over-exfoliating. It is best to use an exfoliating product that contains alpha-hydroxy acids (AHA) or beta-hydroxy acids (BHA) twice a week. The difference between AHA and BHA is a simple but significant one. AHA is water-soluble, whereas BHA is oil-soluble and penetrates the skin through our sebaceous glands (Brooks, 2022). It is advisable to reduce the usage of scrubs as they have a tendency to damage the skin. Exaggerated cleaning and exfoliation strip the skin's natural protection and encourages acne and pimples to form.

- **Be wary of steam:** Saunas and steam rooms are wonderful to remove toxins from the skin, but they can damage the delicate skin on the face. This is especially true for individuals with sensitive skin and those living with rosacea. Steam can damage the acid mantle, leading to moisture loss and encouraging flaccidity.

- **Be careful with treatments:** The type of treatment you use can have a significant impact on the health of your skin. Alcohol-containing products have a tendency to strip the acid mantle, whereas acne treatments tend to be abrasive. It is best to look for treatment products that contain ceramides, as they are gentler alternatives.

- **Avoid SLS:** Cleaners with sodium sulfate or sodium laureth sulfate are not suitable to use on the skin. It strips the skin bare, leaving it feeling stiff. This is not surprising, considering SLS is commonly used in floor cleaners and engine degreasers! If you really love a good lather, look for products that make use of fatty acids or that are plant-based.

- **Over-cleansing in the morning:** Most of the time, a gentle rinse with lukewarm water followed by some micellar water is enough to remove oiliness. If your skin is oily or acne prone, use a gentle cleanser designed for your skin type. Regular bar soaps are one of the worst things we can use on our skin, as they tend to contain SLS, which strips the skin bare.

- **Avoid overstimulating dirty skin:** Massaging the face when you have makeup on is a very bad idea. That's because dirt can become trapped in the pores, leading to the formation of acne and pimples. When cleansing our faces, do so with a gentle massage. This will help to stimulate circulation and improve the appearance of the skin. Ideally, this cleansing massage should be no longer than five minutes.

- **Avoid washing your hair last:** Most shampoos contain sulfates. These ingredients can be quite irritating and may encourage breakouts. It is best to wash your hair first before washing the face and body, as our natural oils will provide a degree of protection against the harsh ingredients in shampoo.

- **Don't forget the toner:** Toners are wonderful products for the skin. Their most important function is to restore the pH balance, thus protecting the acid mantle and the overall health of the skin.

When we neglect to protect and nourish the skin, its protective barrier becomes weak and thin. This often leads to irritation and the accelerated loss of collagen, otherwise known as accelerated aging. Keep in mind that our bodies start to lose collagen in our 30s, but the effect is usually only noticeable several years later (*What Happens to Collagen as We Age*, 2020). It is a natural process, but some bad habits can speed up the process. This is why proper skincare plays a vital role in maintaining the youthful radiance of our skin.

The pH of our skincare and cosmetic products needs to be considered as well, especially when making our own. A simple pH strip can be used to test the acidity or alkalinity of a product. Normally, pH strips will turn different shades of red and orange if a product is acidic or blue and green if a product is alkaline. If a product that we prepare falls in the alkaline range (the test strip turns blue or green), the pH will need to be lowered. This can be done by adding a few drops of citric acid or lactic acid *(La piel y el pH-medición, escala y cosméticos*, 2021). If the pH is too acidic (the test strip is red or orange) the pH can be raised with an alkali like bicarbonate. It should be diluted and added in little drops until the derided pH is obtained. The table below shows the recommended pH levels of typical skincare products:

Product	Recommended pH Level
Exfoliants containing Alpha Hydroxy Acids	3–4
Moisturizers	5–7
Cleansers	4.5–7
Serums	4–6
Toners	5–7

Proper pH levels in our skincare products ensures that the lipid barrier remains intact and that moisture is retained in the skin. This results in skin that is stronger and more resilient when faced with external pollutants and irritants. Daytime moisturizing creams and gels help to protect the skin against pollution, weather, and chemicals found in makeup. Repairing creams and nourishing gels are most effective when the skin relaxes and rests, and are best used at night.

The formulations you'll discover in this book are hypoallergenic and contain minimal preservatives. The tiny doses of preservatives used in the formulations are enough to preserve our cosmetic creations' integrity, protecting them from deterioration by external agents. Additionally, we have the option to control the amount of fragrance, or we can omit it completely without impacting the integrity of the product. In Chapter 5, we'll take a closer look at natural preservative alternatives that you can use if your skin is prone to allergic reactions or irritation. It makes business sense for commercial product brands to store their stock on a large scale, but that also means that they tend to use high concentrations of preservatives. This disqualifies most of these products from the hypoallergenic classification, and when hypoallergenic products come to market, they tend to be pricey.

So it makes sense on two levels to create our own products. First, we know exactly what goes inside the product, so there are no nasty surprises for our delicate skin. Secondly, making our own products can be more cost-effective. As a bonus, if you develop a knack for creating skin-loving products, it can turn into a lucrative side hustle. But before we get ahead of ourselves, we'll need to learn more about the work center and supplies we'll need, a topic we'll cover in the next chapter.

2
Work Center and Supplies

N ow that we have a better understanding of the basic needs of our skin based on its type and pH, we can take the first step towards creating healthy skin-loving products that will delay the effects of aging. Don't worry, creating these products won't cut into your travel budget. Speaking of travel, you might be surprised to learn that Hispanics have impressive buying power, roughly $1.5 trillion in 2019, of which we collectively spent $73 billion on travel (Saffari, 2019). The top products traveling Hispanics tend to buy includes appliances, clothing, footwear, electronics, and cosmetic products (Ruiz, 2016). So learning how to create your own, quality cosmetics can free up a bit more of that travel budget!

In Chapter 6, we'll take a look at a wide variety of botanical extracts and how they can be used as active ingredients in the products that we create. Cosmetic-grade botanical extracts are relatively easy to find in the current marketplace, but we can channel our inner DIY-diva and create these ingredients easily from scratch. Using botanical extracts that we create ourselves tend to have a more significant impact on the skin. I've created botanical extracts for several years and used them to create cosmetics and treat my patients. The results speak for themselves! In this book, you'll find all the best plants and fruits we can use to create extracts for use in cosmetics. These extracts can be adapted and combined according to your skin's needs.

Generally, all skincare and cosmetic products contain the same basic components. We only need to compare the ingredients of our favorite skincare brands to see that this is true. Yes, even that miracle cream your *tía* recommended has the same basic components! The important thing is the quality of the raw material used. We need to ensure that we are using the best quality possible when creating our own products. Quality ingredients are what set most celebrity skincare brands apart from dodgy drugstore brands.

Speaking of skincare brands, in 2022, the worldwide revenue from the sale of cosmetics was projected to be well over $100 billion, with the US market accounting for $18 billion of this revenue (Killip, 2022). This growth is partly due to the cosmetic industry's ability to reinvent itself and use emerging technologies. In fact, the cosmetics industry is one of the few industries that have beaten the 2008 global financial crisis and has continued to grow stronger year after year (Williams, 2016). What can I say? We love our skincare brands so much that we are willing to save them from the dark pit of recession!

Another factor influencing the strong growth of cosmetics is the increased life expectancy and current forms of consumption by new generations. All of this translates to a potentially highly profitable business based on demand and mass consumption. Naturally, we may wonder where we should start in the process of creating our own cosmetics.

· ♥ · ♥ · ♥ · ♥ · ♥ ·

Understanding Cosmetic Ingredients

A good starting point is to become familiar with common ingredients used in cosmetic formulations. All cosmetic formulations are composed of excipients, active ingredients, and additives. These ingredients have specific functions and complement each other to create the desired product. I'll explain each of these ingredients below.

- **Excipients:** This is the component in cosmetics in which our active ingredients are dissolved or mixed. It serves as a vehicle for the use of the product and gives it shape as well as the final appearance. Excipients can be combined to achieve a derided texture. The most commonly used excipient is water, however, alcohol, propylene glycol, glycerin, surfactants, and acetones may be necessary, depending on the product that we are creating.

- **Active ingredient:** This ingredient is responsible for the care of our skin and the effect of what we want to achieve with the product, for example, anti-aging, skin brightening, moisturizing, etc. Active ingredients are the main ingredient of the product and are present in small quantities. There are two reasons for this. Firstly, active ingredients are highly concentrated, so a little bit goes a long way. Secondly, active ingredients can be quite pricey, so we don't want to waste precious ingredients by using more than what is necessary. Extracts, acids, and peptides are examples of active ingredients commonly used to achieve a tightening effect in skin care products. Formulations can have more than one active ingredient to complement the product's benefits. Also, we should keep in mind that active ingredients are not set in stone. What is an active ingredient in one product may be an excipient or additive in another product.

- **Additives:** Additives are not essential to the formulation of cosmetic products, but they improve the final presentation by giving color, aroma, and protecting the product from premature deterioration. In the additive category, we'll find antimicrobial preservatives (which prevent the formation of fungi and bacteria in cosmetic products), dyes (which give the product color), and perfumes that give the final product a pleasant scent.

· ❤ · ❤ · ❤ · ❤ · ❤ ·

Setting up Your Workstation

Now that we have a better understanding of the common ingredients in cosmetic formulations, we can proceed to the second step: Ensuring our workstation is up to the task. This section will help you figure things out, so you can create cosmetic formulations like a pro.

In DIY cosmetics manufacture, we need a dedicated space and a few simple utensils. The ideal is to dedicate a small room to our cosmetic creations. Don't try to create cosmetics in the kitchen, unless you want your creams and gels to be infused with *abuela's* cooking! Here's a pro-tip: Always keep your cosmetics equipment separate and use them exclusively for cosmetics manufacture. Doing so ensures your creations are free from unnecessary contaminants that can impact the quality and purity of the product. Keep things practical by starting with basic equipment. You can always add new materials as you gain experience and confidence in your creations.

Worktable and Storage

A dedicated space is necessary to start our journey into making cosmetics. At the very least, you'll need a clean, flat surface or table to work on. The space you choose to work in must be free from drafts and dampness. You'll need a cupboard and small boxes to keep ingredients organized and easily accessible.

Scale

In most liquids, apart from water and hydrosols, one milliliter does not equal one gram. That's because liquids have different densities. For this reason, we should always weigh out ingredients, including liquids. When using a formula in percentage by weight, we need to keep in mind that the weight of all the ingredients we are using in that formula adds up to 100 grams. Some formulas may be unstable when the ratio of ingredients is off, so weighing ingredients eliminates a lot of potential problems.

It is best to gain experience by creating small batches of each formula, so you'll need a small, sensitive scale. The ideal scale should be able to weigh a minimum of 0.1 grams and a maximum of one kilogram. These scales can be pricey, but a practical and economical option would be to invest in a small, sensitive kitchen scale. This scale should be able to weigh a minimum of 0.01 grams and a maximum of 100 grams.

Coffee Grinder

Coffee grinders are the tools of choice when it comes to making cosmetic powders. The coffee grinder should be used exclusively for your cosmetics laboratory.

Stirring and Mixing

Glass whisks and spatulas with a spoon are irreplaceable tools. Opt for metallic ones when the opportunity arises. Silicone spatulas are useful in the packaging process and help us empty the preparation glass thoroughly, preventing wastage.

Blenders and Hand Mixers

Blenders are used to improve the texture and sensation of a product, increasing the stability thereof. You'll need a blender with most emulsifiers.

For small amounts of 100 grams and under, it is best to use a mini blender for cosmetics. A coffee frother can be used as a substitute in this case. The only drawback is that a coffee frother may stop when blending thick creams. To prevent this, make sure the batteries are well charged beforehand.

For larger quantities (500 grams and above) kitchen blenders are best suited. The immersion blender is the ideal tool in this case and often comes with accessories. The grinder can be used in the manufacture of cosmetic powders, whereas the propeller can emulsify creams. Some blenders come with a homogenizer attachment. This can be used to make silky smooth creams. The attachment is usually quite large and can be used to make large batches (a kilogram or more) of cream at a time.

Hand mixers are useful to mix powders into bath bombs, gels, solid shampoos, scrubs, liquid shampoos, and creams.

Dedicated Heat Tools

A hot plate or ceramic hob is used for various oils, waxes, butters, and essential oils. For the sake of safety, never use an open flame around these ingredients, as they are combustible. Nothing special is needed here, a ceramic hob or hot plate will work perfectly. If you have your heart set on getting a dedicated heat tool for your cosmetics labs, opt for a glass ceramic hot plate. It makes cleanup a breeze.

Pans will be necessary as well, especially when preparing large batches of product. Pants with tall sides can help prevent a lot of spills and messes. Additionally, we can use them to make a bain-marie when heating ingredients.

Glass should not be exposed to direct heat, as the base will become much hotter than the rest of the vessel, overheating the ingredients therein. For this reason, a water bath or bain-marie will become an indispensable tool when creating cosmetic products. We can heat ingredients in microwaves in a pinch, but it is not advised. Microwaves do not heat ingredients evenly, leaving cold spots in some areas and overheating others.

When ointments, solid balms, and creams are prepared hot, we'll need a thermometer to get an accurate temperature reading. There are many different models available on the market. Rod thermometers and digital ones tend to be cheap, but they take longer to get a temperature reading. If using these, you'll need to keep the device clean. The fastest are infrared thermometers, and they tend to be more accurate. The added bonus is that there are no metal rods that need to be cleaned between readings.

Beakers

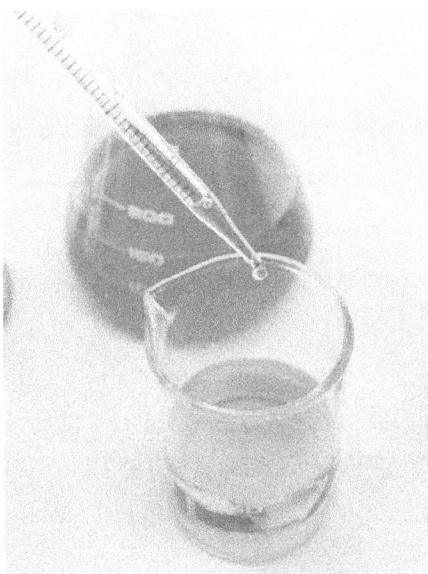

When creating certain products, we may need to heat the ingredients, making the quality of beakers very important. Make sure the beakers you intend to use are made of glass, ideally Pyrex or a suitable alternative such as Duran or borosilicate. Of these, borosilicate glass beakers are the easiest to find. The type of glass the beaker is made of will be indicated on the item. For small batches (100 grams), we'll use a range of beakers frequently. Beaker volumes of 50ml, 100ml, 250ml, and 500ml will be very useful. These beakers tend to be cheap, so it's a good idea to stock up. Here's a hint: When beaker shopping, look for tall and spouted beakers. They pour better!

Mixing Bowls, Liquids, and Packaging Tools

A range of bowls that can accommodate volumes between 300 ml and 2 liters are going to prove very useful. These bowls will come in handy when preparing bath bombs, solid shampoos, or when mixing powders. Regular kitchen bowls are suitable to use.

Plastic pipettes are practical and can be reused until they break. Don't worry, they tend to last a long time and should be cleaned with alcohol. For light liquids and essential oils, look for 1ml pipettes. For extracts, the 3ml pipettes come in handy. Viscous ingredients always leave something behind in a pipette, so be careful. For viscous ingredients, syringes are best.

Syringes are extremely useful when creating cosmetics. We can use syringes to adjust the weight of ingredients accurately. Opt for syringes with plastic plungers if they are more durable. Rubber-tipped plungers eventually swell and break, especially when we use the syringe a lot for essential oils, extracts, and other liquid ingredients. Syringe capacity varies, but 2ml, 5ml, and 10ml syringes are used the most.

Funnels are useful to fill bottles. Nothing special is needed here, plastic or stainless steel funnels (one small and one medium-sized) will get the job done. Using a funnel is way more reliable (and less messy) than eye-balling liquids into a bottle.

Pastry bags come in handy when we need to package thick creams without getting any air pockets. The pastry bag should reach the bottom of the container, filling it evenly. Plastic pastry bags, although disposable, can be reused. When reusing these bags, make sure to clean them thoroughly to remove all traces of the product.

pH Indicators

As we already discovered, the pH of the products we create is crucial as they can have an impact on our skin's overall health. Fortunately, pH papers and strips are affordable and fast-acting tools we can use. These strips can measure pH between different ranges. Generally, pH paper measuring the full range (pH of 1–14) and a mid-range (pH of 4–8) will be used the most in cosmetic preparations. Test strips or indicator strips tend to deliver more accurate pH readings than testing papers.

Packaging and Labeling Considerations

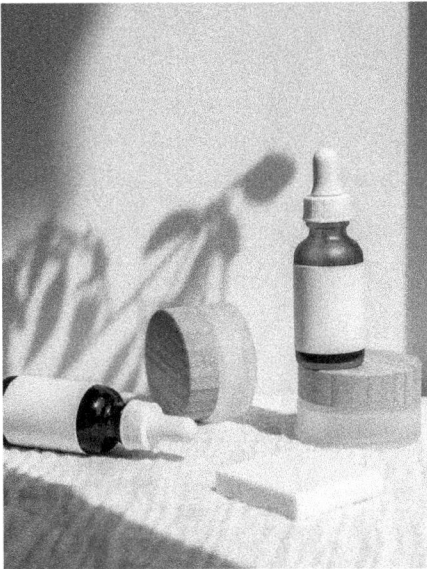

An assortment of bottles and containers will be needed to package and store cosmetics and ingredients. Blue, amber, or black bottles are preferred as they provide better protection for cosmetic ingredients from light. Plastic containers and bottles are commonly used, but aluminum and glass are good great options, too. Different-sized bottles and jars will be needed, the most common volumes you'll come to rely on are 20ml,

50ml, and 100ml. Have a good selection of bottles and jars on hand: spray bottles, dosing pumps, and molds for lipsticks and solid bars.

Make a habit of it to label each bottle with the contents and date of manufacture. Keep in mind that vegetable oils and essential oils can erase some inks, so it is best to use permanent markers on the label.

Protective Equipment and Disinfection

Accidents and spills can happen, but an apron or lab coat will help to save your wardrobe. Nobody wants mica or oily ingredients spilling onto their favorite top! It is a good idea to wear a disposable sanitary cap as well to prevent any stray hairs from ending up in that cream you've been working so hard on. When making solid shampoos, bath bombs, or when we are mixing powders, it is best to have gloves, safety glasses, and a mask on hand. Powdered surfactants can irritate our eyes and mucous membranes. Keep a roll of kitchen paper close by, it will be more useful than you think.

Keeping your work surfaces and equipment clean and disinfected is a crucial step! Natural cosmetics may contain extracts, juices, and other ingredients in which microorganisms may develop. For this reason, hygiene measures and the regular disinfection of equipment used are essential. This helps to eliminate possible microbes and contaminants in the materials we are using, resulting in a higher-quality cosmetic product.

For a thorough clean, it is advised to wash the materials. From here, the materials can be stored in a box until needed. With the next use, spray materials with a strong alcohol spray. To make the spray, dilute seven parts of high-proof alcohol in three parts of water. Allow the materials to air dry before using. Vodka is not strong enough to use for this purpose. Alternatively, materials can be immersed in a liquid material sterilant (follow the vendor's instructions for best results). Always try to create cosmetics in a draft-free space to reduce the chance of contamination. Work surfaces should be cleaned with soap and water, followed by a sterilizing spray of alcohol.

· ❤ · ❤ · ❤ · ❤ · ❤ ·

Ingredients Needed for a Cosmetics Lab

Having the right equipment is important when setting up your workspace, and the same care and consideration should be extended to the ingredients used. Good cosmetics can be produced with simple ingredients. Learning how to preserve ingredients is key to creating long-lasting, quality products. To extend the shelf-life of products, we need to add preservatives, especially when we intend to sell our creations. Always check the technical sheets of preservatives and synthetic ingredients that you want to use to get a good understanding of the ingredient's properties and possible substitutes. These products and raw materials can generally be stored in a cool, dry place that is away from direct sunlight. Cosmetic products are created for different purposes, so the ingredients can vary.

Natural cosmetics ingredients can be organized into two broad categories, i.e. structural and active ingredients. Structural ingredients are emulsifiers, thickeners, oils, pH correctors, stabilizers, hydrosols, preservatives, and distilled water. Active ingredients include vitamins, antioxidants, and sunscreens.

In these formulations, the structural ingredients serve as a transporter for the active ingredients, helping them to reach the skin. The structural ingredients are also responsible for the extensibility, viscosity, and sensation of the product on our skin. There is no shortage of choice with all the different products available in the market!

· ♥ · ♥ · ♥ · ♥ · ♥ ·

Understanding the Solubility of Ingredients

The success of our end product often depends on how well we know our solubles. Knowing which ingredients are water- or oil-soluble can save us a lot of failed batches. This section will teach you everything you need to know about the topic.

Water Soluble

Ingredients in this category can be heated to 70ºC. Water is a common solvent in natural cosmetics and can be used with other water-based ingredients. We can easily use water, hydrosols, aloe vera gel, and other water-soluble ingredients in the same formulation. Here's a list of water-soluble ingredients that are commonly used:

- **Hydrosols/Hydrolates:** These ingredients are used to partially or completely replace distilled water. We use hydrosols to prepare toners, body gels, shampoos, and emulsions. Hydrosols are commonly through distillation with water or steam from different kinds of plant materials.

- **Moisturizers:** Their purpose is to help the skin retain water. Glycerin, urea, sorbitol, sodium lactate, hyaluronic acid, and betaine are commonly used moisturizing ingredients. These ingredients are best used in formulas with an aqueous phase. Cosmetics manufacture involves different phases, but those are explained a little later.

- **Thickeners:** Hydrophilic thickeners are what give body gels, serums, shampoos, and emulsions their texture and viscosity. Xanthan gum, tara gum, guar gum, sclerotium, carboxymethylcellulose, hydroxyethylcellulose, or hydroxypropylmethylcellulose are commonly used.

- **Surfactants:** These ingredients cleanse our skin and hair. They are commonly used in shampoo, shower gels, and micellar water. Cocoglucoside, decylglucoside, and coconut betaine (Cocamidopropyl betaine) are commonly used ingredients.

Oil Soluble

The ingredients in this category have an emollient effect, lending flexibility and softness to the skin. Ingredients are typically vegetable oils or butters.

- **Vegetable oils:** Are often used in facial and body oils, ointments, serums, and creams. Food oils such as sunflower, soybean, coconut, or olive oil are commonly used. Other vegetable oils include fractionated coconut, macadamia and nut oils, blackberry, and jojoba.

- **Butters:** These ingredients take longer to be absorbed by the skin and provide a deeper moisturizing effect. The downside is that they may leave a greasy sensation behind. The most common butters used are shea, cocoa, mango, babassu, and avocado. Butters can be used with oils in the same cosmetic formulation, but they need to be heated beforehand to blend evenly.

Fatty Thickeners and Waxes

These ingredients are very thickening and are commonly used in ointments and stick products. These ingredients can also be used to make creams and oils a thicker consistency. Commonly used waxes include bee, rice, soy, carnauba, and candelilla. Thickeners that are favored include cetearyl alcohol, cetyl alcohol, cetyl palmitate, and stearic acid as they impart a less greasy feel to the product.

Emulsifiers

These ingredients are crucial when we need to make milks and creams. To simplify the process, we can make use of pre-made self-emulsifying bases. This gives us the freedom to focus our attention on the selection of active ingredients. Keep the vendor's specifications in mind when creating products. The goal is to maintain the stability and consistency of the end product. Most pre-made formulations are easy to recognize: They are white, solid, and skin-loving.

Heat Labile Ingredients

Ingredients in this category should be kept safe from high temperatures. Vitamins, antioxidants, and preservatives are some of the ingredients that fall into this category.

- **Antioxidants, chelators, and buffers:** These ingredients are necessary when a formula is at risk of autoxidation. This is when oxidation occurs without any extra help from our side. Juices, pigments, and vitamins are some of the ingredients that fall in this category. Chelators are responsible for removing heavy metals that may contaminate a formulation, while buffers help to keep the pH of an emulsion stable. Water-soluble ingredients that are used in this way include citric acid, lactic acid, sodium gluconate, phytic acid, and vitamin B3. Vitamin E acetate is a special antioxidant, being fat-soluble, and often used to extend the shelf life of butters and oils.

- **Essential oils:** These provide aroma and many powerful cosmetic properties. Aroma is a matter of personal taste, but it can be one of the most complicated things to adjust in natural cosmetics. Each ingredient contributes something to the smell of the end product. Popular essential oils used in cosmetics include rose, geranium, tangerine, lemon, bergamot, rosemary, ylang-ylang, and rosewood. When adding essential oils to a formulation, do so little by little, otherwise your product could smell very overpowering.

- **pH regulators:** The pH of most cosmetics need to be adjusted. To lower the pH of a formulation, lactic acid and citric acid are used. Dilute in water at a ratio of 20-50% and add one drop at a time when adjusting pH. To raise the pH, caustic soda, caustic potash, and bicarbonate are used. Dilute at a ratio of 20-50% in water and use one drop at a time to adjust the pH.

- **Plant extracts:** The ingredients in this category have beneficial cosmetic properties. Normally glyceric extracts, dry extracts, or oleates are used. If using dry extracts, keep in mind that it must be previously dissolved in a small amount of water or hydrosol before adding it to the formulation. There are many types of plant extracts to choose from, so select the ones that are appropriate for the type of cosmetic you'd like to create.

- **Preservatives:** Crucial in cosmetics that have an aqueous phase. Products that contain juices, plant extracts, and herbal teas need preservatives as they can easily be contaminated with mold and bacteria. It is best to add preservatives to your cosmetics after the pH has been adjusted, and the emulsion is cooled to 45ºC. The most commonly used preservatives include benzoic acid and sodium benzoate (0.1-0.5%), benzyl alcohol (0.3-1%), sorbic acid (0.1-0.5%), and potassium sorbate (0.1-0. 3%).

- **Vitamins:** These ingredients are non-negotiable and cannot be missing in your formulations. They are regenerative, skin-protecting, and antioxidant ingredients. All vitamins are usually added in the thermolabile phase of manufacture, but there are some exceptions. Vitamin B3, A, and C palmitate have high melting points and are fat soluble. Due to their heat-resistant nature, it is best to add them to the hot oil phase of manufacture. I'll clarify the different phases of cosmetic production soon.

- **Specific action assets:** These ingredients are used to enhance the action of a cosmetic. Skin whitening, antioxidants, skin firming and anti-wrinkle formulations are some functions we can add to cosmetics with these ingredients. Some common examples are coenzyme Q10, caffeine, activated ceramide, kojic acid, and allantoin. Refer to your supplier/vendor's instructions for the proper use and dosage of these ingredients.

Phases of Cosmetic Production

Many cosmetic formulations are made by creating emulsions (a mixture of oil and water). The process typically starts with heating the water-soluble ingredients to a temperature between 75-80 °C. This is the water phase. Depending on the product we are making, we may need to premix a thickener to add to the water along with the other ingredients.

The oil phase starts in a separate vessel. Ingredients in this vessel are heated to 75-80°C, this includes emulsifiers and emollients. These heating and mixing steps in the oil phase often make use of a propeller impeller to deliver a homogenized final product.

When the water- and oil-soluble ingredients are heated, they can be combined to create an emulsion. As soon as we achieve an even blend in the product, it can be cooled by stirring. After the ingredients have been cooled to a certain temperature, the remaining ingredients can be added to finish the product. This includes preservatives, fragrances, and pH adjustments. I've broken down the steps we need to take to form a foolproof emulsion below:

- **Aqueous phase:** This is often the first step and involves water-soluble ingredients being heated to temperature.

- **Oil phase:** This is the second step. Here we heat fat-soluble ingredients, emollients, or glyceryl stearate to temperature using a separate vessel.

- **Emulsion phase:** When both water- and oil-soluble ingredients are heated, we can combine them to create an emulsion. Use a propeller impeller to mix the liquids into a homogeneous blend for at least 20 minutes (*Emulsion Mixing with Cosmetics*, n.d.)

- **Cool down phase:** This is the fourth step. After mixing the emulsion for 20 minutes, the propeller impeller can be replaced with an anchor impeller. This helps the mixture cool down evenly. Continue mixing the emulsion until it cooled to 30 °C.

- **Temperature-sensitive ingredients:** When the mixture is cooled, we can add temperature-sensitive ingredients such as preservatives, coloring, and fragrances to the product.

- **pH adjustment:** This is the last step. Test the product and adjust the pH as needed to finalize the product.

Follow these steps every time, and you'll be well on your way to creating dreamy and creamy emulsions. After this chapter, you should be almost ready to start creating quality cosmetics. Now all you need is a solid understanding of cosmetic chemistry and the principles that underpin it, a topic that we'll explore in the next chapter.

·❤·❤·❤·❤·❤·

3
Principles of Cosmetic Chemistry

In the previous chapter, we took a close look at the ingredients we'll need for different cosmetic products. As we know, cosmetic products have different textures and forms. Each of these textures tells us something about the ratio of the ingredients used in the end product. There are different cosmetic forms, but the ones we'll deal with regularly are as follows:

- **Aqueous solutions (hydrophilic):** These are liquid products, usually a solvent, in which other components are dissolved. Water is frequently a component in these solutions, as in the case of essences, foam cleansers, and toners.

- **Oily solutions (lipophilic):** These liquids are oily to the touch, such as facial oils and cleansing oils, and balms.

- **Gels:** These semi-solid products have a fresh texture. Examples here include creams in a gel format and aloe vera gel. Gels are actually liquids with a gelling agent. This gelling agent acts as a net, trapping water molecules and keeping the liquid suspended. The amount and type of gelling agent will impact the viscosity of the end product.

- **Emulsions:** These are mixtures of water-based and oily ingredients with the help of emulsifiers. The texture of an emulsion can vary, ranging from light to luxuriously rich, and isn't dependent on the ingredients that we use. Emulsions are useful to provide the skin with moisture, prevent moisture loss, and can deliver emollients to the skin.

Cosmetics can take different forms, so we need to keep in mind that the ingredient function can change as well. Vitamin C is a good example of this. In one formulation, it can be used as an antioxidant, whereas another formulation might use it as an additive instead.

· ♥ · ♥ · ♥ · ♥ · ♥ ·

Understanding Cosmetic Components

There are many active ingredients that we can use in cosmetic solutions, including softeners, conditioners, abrasives, detergents, sunscreens, dyes, pigments, and perfumes. Some of the most commonly used ingredients include oat extract, menthol, zinc stearate, lanolin, calcium carbonate, carbon dioxide silica, glycerol, and ascorbic acid.

Apart from the active ingredients, the excipient used is the second most important ingredient in a cosmetic formulation. Excipients can be made up of one or more substances in which all the ingredients of the cosmetic are mixed, so it stands to reason that the excipient needs to be compatible with our ingredients. The most commonly used excipient is water, but fatty substances are used as well. Water, oil, and fat are gentle on the skin, being fully compatible with our skin's natural secretion of water and sebum.

Excipients can fulfill different roles, acting as active ingredients, correctors, or additives in different products. For example, acetone in nail polish remover is both an active ingredient and solvent. In another example, lanolin can often be found as an active ingredient in nourishing masks, but it can be used as a viscosity corrector in moisturizing creams. It all depends on the excipient used. Broadly speaking, when the excipient used is mainly water, we can expect the cosmetic to have a liquid appearance. With fats and oils as excipients, cosmetics adopt a denser feel and appearance. Excipients can be quite complex, some can be monophasic while others are polyphasic. Let's take a closer look at the differences between the two.

- **Monophasic excipients:** Here the liquid contains two main components (the solute and solvent). The substances disperse evenly in the excipient, forming a homogeneous solution. Distilled water is an excellent example of a monophasic excipient.

- **Polyphasic excipients:** Gels, emulsions, moisturizing creams, and masks all necessitate the use of an emulsifier or surfactant to obtain the desired end result and are known as polyphasic excipients. Yes, that serum we sometimes scrape out of our favorite face mask packet counts as a polyphasic excipient.

Additives

Additives are ingredients used to preserve, perfume, and color cosmetic products. They are not crucial to the formulation and function of the cosmetic, but can help to increase the product's durability and attractiveness. So they can be a pretty big deal when marketing cosmetic products. Antimicrobials, antioxidants, and alcohol are among the most frequently used additives in cosmetic products. Their purpose is to help preserve the active ingredients used in the cosmetics and to prevent the overall decay of the product.

Additives are also used to give color and scent to a product. Keep in mind, there needs to be an association between the color and scent of your cosmetic creations. This is why lotions and creams with a light pink color always have a musk, rose, or strawberry scent. Just imagine what your reaction would be if you came across a purple-colored cream that smelled of oranges! *¡Ay! ¡Qué susto!*

We've come to associate certain scents with certain colors, so pairing a scent and color needs to make sense. Additives may trigger allergies, so use them carefully when formulating cosmetics. Take a closer look at the label of your favorite cosmetic. You may notice that additives and correctors are indicated strangely. These ingredients will either be indicated by name or with an *E* followed by a number. Generally, those E-numbers mean the following:

- E-100 to E-200: The ingredient used is food coloring.

- E-200 to E-300: These ingredients are antimicrobial.

- E-300 to E-400: The ingredients used are antioxidants, stabilizers, and emulsifiers.

- E-400 to E-500: Ingredients used are emulsifiers and thickeners.

Correctors

These ingredients modify the formula of our cosmetic creations. We use these ingredients to make cosmetic formulas more stable, and it makes the product easier to apply. Typical correctors include viscosity modifiers, solubilizers, softeners, pH correctors, and metal ion sequestrants.

Viscosity modifiers help to improve the texture of a product, making it easier to apply and use. In many aqueous solutions, carbopol is often used to adjust viscosity. In oily solutions, we tend to use cellulose or substances that can absorb fat to improve texture. Metal ion sequestrants, like ethylenediaminetetraacetic acid (EDTA), are widely used to bind iron and calcium ions, preserving the function and appearance of the cosmetic. It is also used to counter any hardness in water when formulating rinse-off products (*EDTA*, n.d.).

Solubilizers and solvents make it possible for fats and oils to be evenly dispersed in a cosmetic formula by surfactants. Surfactants may cause some of the ingredients to dissolve in the excipient, especially when isopropyl or alcohol is used. Softeners and emollients help to restore the balance of a formula, especially when we make use of ingredients that may remove oil from the skin, such as petrolatum or lanolin.

All the ingredients in a formula have their own task to fulfill, but they all work together in harmony to create a balanced and effective product.

· ❤ · ❤ · ❤ · ❤ · ❤ ·

The Function of Ingredients

Ever wondered why the ingredients list on your favorite cosmetic sometimes includes the letters INCI? INCI is the abbreviation for the International Nomenclature for Cosmetic Ingredients. It is an international system that is used to name cosmetic ingredients. This is done to ensure that people all over the world can read and understand the ingredients on the label, regardless of the language spoken. Think of it as a common language that is used in the cosmetic industry.

All the ingredients in a formulation are necessary. Each formula consists of different parts. The basic part (also called the chassis) defines the basic properties of the cosmetic and helps to keep it stable until the product expires. Some ingredients in the chassis may not have a direct function on our skin, but do have a function in the formula they are used. For example, in many creams, lotions, and gels, we'll find carbomer or acrylates. The main function of these ingredients is to improve the viscosity of the product and ensure that the texture does not change over time. Solvents, preservatives, pH regulators, emulsifiers, chelators, and rheology regulators all form part of a product's chassis and are indispensable when creating cosmetics.

Other ingredients, like natural extracts and certain vegetable oils, can fulfill certain functions on the skin. For example, lavender extracts and oils might be used in formulations aimed to soothe the skin. These ingredients can also fulfill a marketing purpose, making cosmetic products appear more attractive to consumers. This is especially true when the ingredient used is present in the formulation in a lower percentage than its effective dose (*Basic Concepts of Cosmetic Chemistry,* 2019). For example, licorice extract can be useful to combat blemishes when it is present at an effective dose in cosmetic formulations. Added in lower percentages to a cosmetic product, the licorice extract fulfills a marketing purpose, giving the consumer something to connect to when they read the product label.

Perfumes and dyes are used to fulfill a sensory function, that is, the product needs to be pleasing to our eyes and noses. We'd be a lot more hesitant to use cosmetic products if they did not look right or smell nice. The final component, assets or active ingredients, have an effect on the skin. To be effective and safe, cosmetic formulations only incorporate a certain percentage of these ingredients.

· ♥ · ♥ · ♥ · ♥ · ♥ ·

Deciphering Cosmetic Labeling Requirements

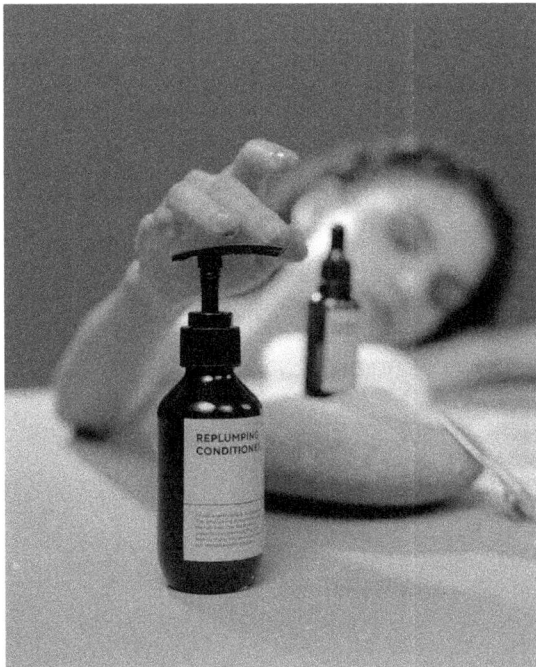

Products go through many stages before they are fit for sale, and an informative label can't be overlooked. When readying your cosmetic products for sale, pay close attention to the label. What is the first thing you see when looking at the label? High-quality pictures and colors are useful to grab a potential customer's attention. This part of the label is referred to as the prime label. These labels are accompanied by secondary, supplemental labels filled with product information. A well-designed label will relay the following information to a potential customer:

- **Ingredients:** Customers can clearly see what ingredients were used to create the product. It is important to display ingredients that may trigger allergic reactions.

- **Health risks:** Labels should always convey if a health risk may arise from the use of the product. Warnings should be clearly displayed.

- **Instructions:** Cosmetics always should come with a set of instructions on how to properly use and store the product. Booklet labels are lifesavers when instructions need to go in-depth.

- **Aesthetics:** Product labels are useful marketing tools all on their own. A potential customer may be attracted to the colors and uniqueness of one label over another, increasing the chances of completing the sales cycle. I found that bold, memorable labels work best.

There's more to labeling than simply relaying product information to consumers. Labeling helps a product stand out, significantly increasing the chances of purchase. Research suggests that up to 85% of shoppers' purchasing decisions are influenced by labels (*Why Is Product Labeling so Important?*, 2017).

There's quite a bit of information we need to add to product labels, but things can become a bit more complicated when selling cosmetic products across borders. In this section, we'll take a closer look at cosmetic labeling requirements according to EU and United States requirements.

EU Labeling Requirements

Regulation 1223/2009 is what we need to pay attention to when we need to comply with EU labeling requirements. The EU developed a specific set of requirements producers of cosmetic goods need to follow if their products are aimed at the EU market.

The container and outer packaging should include all product information. The font used should be legible and, more importantly, indelible. Labels require a lot of information, some of which include:

- Name and address of the responsible person.

- Country of origin.

- Where consumers can find more product information.

- Quantity.

Interestingly, we don't need to indicate expiration dates on cosmetic products with a shelf life of longer than 30 months (Vallez, 2021). It's a different story when labeling single-use products. The expiration date is needed, even if the shelf life is long. The same goes for products that have a low risk of being contaminated by bacteria and fungi.

Labels should clearly indicate if any consumers need to take any precautions during the use of the product. For example, "Avoid contact with eyes." Another important point to note is that ingredients should be listed in descending order of concentration, starting from the highest concentration.

We'll need to comply with language considerations as well, as several countries in the EU have languages different from our own. At the very least, the following information will need to be translated into the official language of the country where your product would be sold:

- Content.

- Special precautions.

- The function of the product.

We'll need to be extra careful with our labels, as the images, texts, brands, and signs used cannot imply a product has additional functions. For example, imaging on an antiaging cream may imply that it can permanently reverse the aging process, a claim that is simply not true. We'll need to back up any claims we make on the labeling to remain on the safe side.

United States Labeling Requirements

Things work a bit differently in the States where labels are concerned. Cosmetic products sold in the United States need to adhere to the rules set out by the Federal Food, Drug, and Cosmetic Act as well as the Correct Packaging and Labeling Act, and regulations set by the FDA under these laws. This means that the sale of misbranded or adulterated cosmetics is strictly prohibited. Regulatory action may ensue when products are identified as misbranded. To avoid this from happening, take a closer look at the label and see if it contains:

- False or misleading information and product claims.

- Identifying information about the manufacturer, distributor, or packer. We are looking for names and addresses here.

Furthermore, United States law is very particular about where on the label certain bits of information appear. Knowing where to place this bit of information is important and requires one to know the difference between an outer and an inner container. In product packaging, the outer container has a main presentation panel along with information panels, whereas the inner counter has a front panel and information panels. To comply with regulations, we'll need to know what information can be printed where, as each panel is dedicated to certain bits of product information.

- **Labeling information on outer packaging:** The following product information needs to appear here: Product name, use of the product, net contents expressed using U.S. units, and warnings.

- **Labeling information on inner packaging:** These segments are reserved for the ingredient list, instructions for use, and warnings where applicable. Additionally, the inner packaging needs to display the business name and location, country of origin, lot number, and expiration date of the product. Information on the label should be in English, with certain exceptions.

Keep in mind that some states may have additional regulations with regard to the sale of cosmetic products. One such example is *Proposition 65* in

California. This document includes a list of chemicals that are known to cause reproductive harm, birth defects, and cancer (Feregotto, 2019). If a product marketed in California contains any of the ingredients mentioned in that list, the label needs to have a clear and reasonable warning. It's a little bit of a headache to go through all these regulations, but it's a necessary evil if we want to market our products in these areas. The sacrifices we make for beauty sometimes!

Up until this point, I've been laying the foundation you'll need to create your own cosmetic products. Now that you've got a better understanding of cosmetic ingredients, safety practices, and the role of pH, the real fun can begin. In the next chapter, you'll learn how to create base materials and much more!

·♥·♥·♥·♥·♥·

4
Manufacture of Basic Products

P reventing the deterioration of a cosmetic product is done by adding preservatives to the mixture. The main function of preservatives is to inhibit the growth of microorganisms that may contaminate or spoil a product. These preservatives are necessary in many cases, as cosmetic products tend to provide microorganisms with a rich and nourishing environment to grow. In this chapter, you'll learn how to create different base products, but before we get there, we need to learn how to preserve cosmetics.

Choosing the right preservative for a cosmetic can be tricky. We need to take the formulation into account as well as the type of consumer the product is aimed at and where on the body the product will be used. As you can see, there is a lot to consider! For this reason, many cosmetic manufacturers use broad-spectrum cosmetic preservatives. These preservatives are formulated to be effective against mold, bacteria, and yeast. Good preservatives are effective at very low concentrations, reducing the chances of producing an allergic reaction or skin irritation.

The preservative that we settle on using needs to be approved by regulating authorities and be compatible with the ingredients used in the formulation. This includes the packaging.

Quality preservatives are stable throughout their shelf life and can withstand different pH levels, temperature, and humidity conditions. On top of this, a quality preservative will not change the organoleptic characteristics (how a product looks, feels, and smells) or the pH of a product. Keep in mind that using cosmetic preservatives is only one step we can take to safeguard the quality of a product. All the raw materials, manufacturing practices, and packaging used to create the final product should work in harmony with the preservative to maintain the best product quality possible.

· ♥ · ♥ · ♥ · ♥ · ♥ ·

Permitted Cosmetic Preservatives

The use of cosmetic preservatives is guided by strict regulation. The main concern of these regulations is consumer safety. For example, Annex V of Regulation 1223:2009 of the European Union specifies a list of cosmetic preservatives that can be used, as well as their maximum concentrations allowed in products (*Regulation (EC) No 1223/2009 of the European Parliament*, 2022). Broadly speaking, cosmetic preservatives can be divided into two groups: Organic acids and alcohols.

- **Organic acids:** The most recognizable preservatives falling in this category are undoubtedly parabens and esters of para-hydroxy-benzoic acid (PHBA). These ingredients are used widely as they demonstrate their efficacy in numerous products. Other preservatives that are commonly used include benzoic acid, dehydroacetic acid, and sorbic acid.

- **Alcohols:** These preservatives act on fats and proteins present in cell membranes, interfering with the cell's metabolism and transportation process. Alcohols and their derivatives also denature proteins, making them a good choice to inhibit microbial growth in cosmetic products. Phenoxyethanol (a phenolic derivative) is one of the most commonly used alcohols to preserve cosmetic preparations.

Sometimes, preservatives are confused with antioxidants or biocides. This misleading information can make its way on the label, potentially confusing the end-user of your product. To clarify: Antioxidants prevent oxidation of ingredients, preservatives prevent microorganisms from growing in the cosmetic product by creating an unfavorable environment for them, and biocides are used to decontaminate a product where micrograms have grown. Keep this important distinction in mind when labeling cosmetic products.

Preservative Alternatives

Preservatives have gained a questionable reputation over the years, giving rise to myths. One of those myths is the belief that all preservatives are bad. "Preservative-free" products are offered as an alternative, but is the issue really that simple? Take a closer look at the products available on the market, you'll notice something interesting on the label. Nearly all water-based products will list a natural or synthetic preservative. That's because these ingredients are necessary to maintain product stability and safety in water-based formulations. Over the years, there has been an increase in demand to use preservatives of natural origin in cosmetic products. I'll share a tip with you: Steer clear from preservative-free, water-based products. They are easy to contaminate, and this makes them a bad choice for the skin.

Some of the commonly used preservatives in this category include organic acids, which are often accompanied by essential oils, polyalcohols, and perfumes. We need to be cautious when using three kinds of preservatives, as high amounts of the ingredient are needed to be effective, increasing the likelihood of allergic reactions and irritation.

The only type of skincare product that can be formulated without preservatives is anhydrous ones (*Tipos de conservantes cosméticos: ¿Qué debes saber sobre ellos?*, 2021). These products contain zero water and are made from plant oils, butters, and waxes. Keep in mind that anhydrous products can and will become contaminated when they come in contact with water. We'll need to be extra mindful of wet fingers introducing contaminants when no preservatives are used.

· ♥ · ♥ · ♥ · ♥ · ♥ ·

Preservative	Reason to Avoid	Used in
Parabens, including Butylparaben, Methylparaben and Propylparaben	Parabens have been found to mimic estrogen in our bodies, making it a risk to human health. Paraben compounds are also believed to contribute to breast tumors and male infertility (Lincho et al., 2021).	Cosmetics, skincare, and personal care products.
Diazolidinyl urea and Imidazolidinyl urea	These preservatives prevent microbial growth by forming formaldehyde. Formaldehyde acts as a preservative, but can trigger skin and eye irritation.	Cosmetic products, pharmaceutical creams, household detergents, and skincare products.
Benzalkonium chloride	This ingredient can be used as a biocide and cationic surfactant, but if used wrongly, benzalkonium chloride may impact the growth of cancer cells (Is Benzalkonium Chloride Safe?, 2022). The ingredient is a known skin- and eye-irritant.	Mainly used in disinfectant products and cleaning supplies.
Triclosan	The use of triclosan is banned due to the health risk this synthetic preservative poses. Research found that the preservative interferes with the functioning of thyroid hormone, making it a possible endocrine disruptor that can lead to	Used in antibacterial soaps, tubes of toothpaste, body washes and cosmetics.

Discovering Different Kinds of Preservatives

We mainly deal with two kinds of preservatives: Synthetic and natural. Part of the reason why preservatives have earned such a questionable reputation is that many synthetic preservatives have been linked to skin irritation. Some preservatives have been found to impact long-term health too, so we need to do our due diligence and research the preservative we intend to use thoroughly. The table below details preservatives we should never use.

Don't let the table fool you, though. Not all preservatives are bad. Some preservatives, like benzyl alcohol, are deemed safe for use under COSMOS Organic Certification criteria (*Preservatives in Skincare: What You Need to Know,* n.d.). Other, generally safe, preservatives generally used in cosmetics include:

- **Phenoxyethanol (PE):** A preservative found naturally occurring in chicory and green tea. A synthetic version is created in labs for cosmetic purposes.

- **Caprylyl glycol:** This alcohol is derived from caprylyl glycol and acts as a humectant and preservative. It tends to be a safer option than most preservatives. The ingredient can be used with other preservatives to increase their antimicrobial activity.

- **Potassium sorbate:** Naturally found in some fruits, a synthetic version is made in labs for cosmetic purposes.

Broad-spectrum preservatives are generally considered safe and protect our cosmetic creations from bacteria, mold, and yeast. You'll often find that cosmetic products contain more than one kind of preservative to achieve broad-spectrum protection.

· ❤ · ❤ · ❤ · ❤ · ❤ ·

Mixing Cosmetic Preservative

Budding entrepreneurs have a wide selection of substances to choose from when it comes to preservatives. Sometimes we select a product purely on because we like the packaging or heard good things about it. This selection process serves us well when we want to make chimichurri and other tasty treats, but is a risky tactic when applied to cosmetic ingredients. Doubly so when choosing preservatives!

When it comes to creating cosmetics, it is imperative that we educate ourselves about the substances that we use. This is a necessity, not only to satisfy our own curiosity, but to empower us with the knowledge to educate our potential customers about the ingredients they read on the label.

One preservative that is popularly used in cosmetic products is Cosgard (also known as Geogard 221). This natural, water-soluble broad-spectrum preservative is produced and patented by Lonza. The product is a harmonious blend of Gluconolactone and Sodium Benzoate (What Is Cosgard (Geogard 221), n.d.). When used in cosmetics, it performs a preservative action by slowly releasing a safe, mild acid known as gluconic acid. The preservative has no noticeable effect on the aroma of the final product, which is part of the reason why it is so widely used. The table below summarizes all the key points we need to know about this preservative.

Important characteristics	Description
International Nomenclature of Cosmetic Ingredients (INCI)	Gluconolactone (and) Sodium Benzoate (and) Calcium Gluconate.
Appearance	A powder that is off-white in color and has a smooth texture.
pH Value	The pH value ranges from 3 to 6. It is advised to use a buffer, as the product can cause the pH values to drop.
Recommended dosage	0.75-2%
Compatibility	The ingredient is compatible with all skin types and works well with a wide range of ingredients. This product can be used in cosmetics that are intended for daily use. Please note, this ingredient is not suited for use in aerosolized products.
Shelf life	The product can last up to two years.
Heat, absorption rate, and storage	The product is designed to be heat-resistant and can be safely used if the cosmetic has a hot water phase. The preservative is absorbed fast and should be stored in a cool, dry and dark place.
Suitable substitute	Liquid Germall Plus

Preservatives have different mechanisms of action in which they prevent microbial development in products. Cosgard works by providing microbiological resistance to bacteria, yeast, and fungus. As a bonus, it provides additional moisturization to the skin, making it an all-round safe and gentle product with no known side effects. This preservative is widely considered to be one of the safest to use in cosmetic products.

It should be noted that Cosgard (Geogard) can only be used in the aqueous phase. The product may take a long time to dissolve if used in cold preparations, but there is a simple solution for this. Add the preservative to a beaker with distilled water, cover the beaker with some cling film to keep contaminants out, and let the product dissolve overnight. The next morning, you'll have a preservative you can easily incorporate into your cosmetic creations.

· ♥ · ♥ · ♥ · ♥ · ♥ ·

Preparing Base Materials

An essential skill we need to master is preparing base materials for our products. The materials we need and prepared active agents (most are identified as botanical extracts) can be sourced from suppliers of raw cosmetic materials. Learning to prepare base materials is a practical step and can help cut the final product's production cost. Remember that the tools and utensils used during cosmetic manufacture should never be used for something else. This is to eliminate the risk of cross-contamination and keep our creations safe to use for longer. All tools, utensils, and surfaces should be clean; it is better if you wash and sterilize them with alcohol for safety, regardless of whether they are new.

You must allocate a specific site for this activity and ensure that your products and raw material are not directly exposed to the sun or high temperatures. Whether you are creating products for personal use, or want to turn your creations into a commercial activity, the materials detailed in this section will serve you well. To create the formulations in this section, you'll need the following work materials:

- Electric burner with one or two burners.

- Hand mixer or for baking.

- Heat-resistant glass container.

- Kitchen thermometer and pH meter.

- Glass mixer or stirring rod.

Base materials are basic, ready-to-use products that we can enrich with our choice of ingredients. When adding additional ingredients to base creams and gels, keep in mind that we need to keep the proportions appropriate. This is important to keep the product functioning optimally and to minimize the risk of skin irritation. The wonderful thing about base materials is that they can be whipped up relatively quickly. Simple and quick to use, they are one of the first avenues I encourage you to explore when entering this exciting world.

· ❤ · ❤ · ❤ · ❤ · ❤ ·

Creating Base Creams

Base creams can be personalized in three simple steps. First, we need to weigh the ingredients. Be sure to respect the quantities and be careful about introducing contaminants. Weigh your prepared base cream and other ingredients in a sterile container. The second step involves adding active ingredients to the base. In this step, we can add fragrance and coloring to the product if desired. In the last step, we'll mix the ingredients until they are completely incorporated into the base and package them in a suitable container. Remember to keep stirring the mixture for a few minutes after all the ingredients are incorporated. This is necessary to ensure all ingredients are fully integrated into the base. From here, we simply check and correct the pH and add preservatives if used.

Basic Cream Base

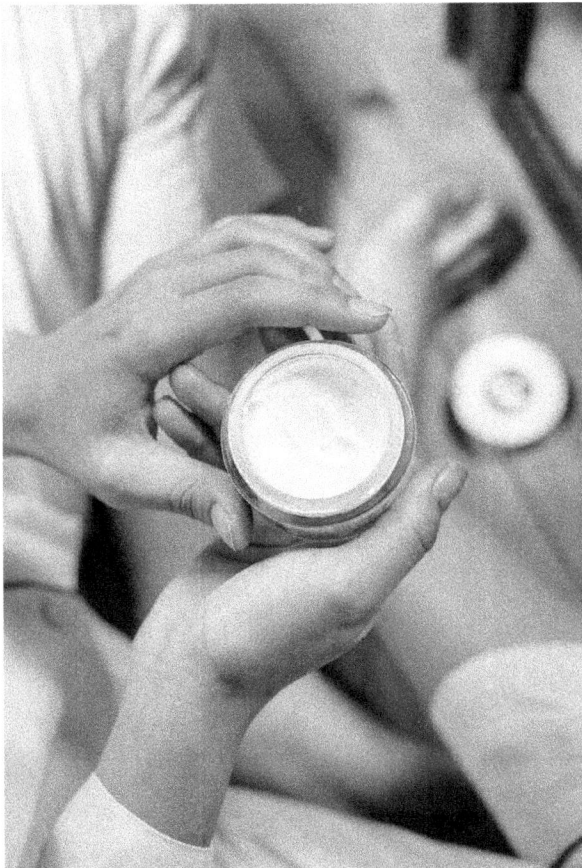

This base cream is light and imparts a silky, velvety texture to the skin. The formulation is easily absorbed by the skin. With this base, we can safely add up to 3% of assets when creating facial and body products (*Cremas base: Qué son, cuál elijo para mi piel y recetas sencillas*, 2021). To make 100g of an enriched cream base, you'll need:

Materials	Quantity 100 ml	Quantity 1 liter
Croda CR2	25 gm	250 gm
Distilled water	71 ml	710 ml
Conservative solution	4 ml	40 ml

Directions:

Preparation is very simple. Melt Crodabase CR2 in a container at 75 to 85ºC. Next, using a separate container, we need to heat water to the same temperature. Now slowly add the Crdodabase to the water by shaking with mechanical help. When a homogenous blend has been created, add the preservative. Remember to keep stirring as the mixture cools, as this will give you the desired product consistency. When the product is cooled, store it in a clean, sterilized container. The base cream is now ready to be used in your cosmetic creations.

· ❤ · ❤ · ❤ · ❤ · ❤ ·

Cosmetic Gel Base

This moisturizing product does not leave a greasy feel on the skin. This gel base also has a thick consistency and high viscosity, making it useful for several cosmetic preparations. Its formulation contains propylene glycol, a component that gives much softness applied to the skin. Being a water-based product, you must use it with the recommended amount of preservatives. Follow the amounts detailed in the table below to create the gel base.

Materials	Quantity 100 ml	Quantity 1 Liter
Carbopol Ultrex 21	1 gm	10 gm
Triethanolamine TEA	1 ml	10 ml
Propilenglicol	6 ml	60 ml
Conservative solution	4 ml	40 ml
Distilled water	88 ml	880 ml

Directions:

Mix the preservative solution with the propylene glycol. Add the distilled water, stirring little by little. In a separate container, you must prepare the gelling base, mixing the carbopol and distilled water until you get a thick consistency. Add the gelling base to the initial mixture. Add the triethanolamine and put it in a container until use. Label and leave the product for 24 hours before use. Store in a clean, fresh, and dry environment.

Xanthan Gum Gel Base

Xanthan gum is becoming an increasingly popular ingredient in gel bases. That's because the gum is a natural gelling agent, making it suitable for use in certified organic cosmetic products. Xanthan gum is generally compatible with most cosmetic active ingredients and can be used as a thickening and stabilizing agent. Keep in mind that the thickness of the gel depends on how much Xanthan gum we use. Formulations usually contain 0.5% to 3% Xanthan gum (*Cómo hacer un gel base con goma Xantana*, 2020). If your gel starts to give you a runny effect after two or three days, you may need to reconsider the quality of the Xanthan gum you are using. To create this gel base, you'll need:

Materials	Quantity 100 ml	Quantity 1 Liter
Distilled water	91 ml	910 ml
Vegetable glycerin	3 ml	30 ml
Xanthan gum	2 gm	20 gm
Preservative solution	4 ml	40 ml

Directions:

Weigh out the vegetable glycerin in a clean glass bowl. Carefully add Xanthan gum to the glycerin and mix to form a gel paste. Next, add the distilled water and stir to incorporate all the ingredients fully. Allow the gel base to rest for a few minutes to thicken. Test the pH and adjust it if needed. Finally, stir in the preservative and transfer the prepared gel base to a suitable container for storage and use.

· ♥ · ♥ · ♥ · ♥ · ♥ ·

Soap Base

When it comes to soap bases, there is no shortage of choice. For predictable results, it is best to use quality soap bases, which we'll investigate closer in this section. We'll be taking a closer look at Texapon, giving you a solid baseline to compare possible substitutes if the need arises.

Texapon is a surfactant found in many cleaning products. The product is a fluid paste with a touch of yellow. It is a high-concentration anionic detergent raw material that can be easily diluted when used correctly (*Texapon,* 2022). Skin generally tolerates the ingredient well, making it compatible with most skin types, and the ingredient's emulsifying and moisturizing properties make it a popular choice in cosmetics. The products have good foaming capacity and can be used with anionic and nonionic surfactants.

The product is mainly used in the production of cleaning agents such as special cleaning agents, multipurpose cleaners, carpet cleaners, etc. It is completely water-soluble. As a bonus, we can use Texapon during the cold steps of cosmetic production, making it quite a versatile ingredient. When using this product, we'll need to be careful not to agitate the liquid too much when dissolving it. This way we'll avoid creating excessive foam.

A good soap base product will have a good foaming effect, even when dissolved at low temperatures, excellent detergent powder, hard water resistance, good moisturizing, and emulsifying properties, be compatible with different skin types, and can be used in the formation of many different products (shampoos, toothpaste, etc.) (*Texapon Liquido,* 2021). It is a tall order, which is why the quality of soap bases matters. I'll share a simple, liquid soap base we can use when making most shampoos and detergents.

Materials	Quantity 1 liter
Texapon 70/SG	400 ml
Distilled water	600 ml

Directions:

Combine ingredients in a glass mixing bowl carefully without foaming until partially incorporated. Leave this mixture to rest for 24 hours and mix again carefully until the mixture is fully incorporated. Pour the soap base into a clean bottle for storage. Remember to add a label indicating the name of the product created and the date.

·❤·❤·❤·❤·❤·

Preparing Extracts

Plants house many substances (phytochemicals) which are beneficial for the skin. One of the easiest ways we can incorporate nature's goodness into cosmetic products is by adding botanical extracts to the formulation. These extracts are relatively easy to find, or they can be prepared at home. Preparing botanical extracts at home has the additional benefit of customization, as we can select and pair extracts to create unique products. Before we get excited about the possibilities, it is necessary to clarify what botanical extracts are.

Botanical extracts are active products derived from plant material through the use of solvents. Extracts for cosmetic use are made with macerates, which contain beneficial properties for the skin. To prepare extracts, it is best to use dried plant material. The reason is twofold. Firstly, using dried plant materials minimizes any water content in the formulation, this helps to reduce the risk of spoilage. Secondly, it is practical. Using dried plant materials enables us to use accurate amounts with every preparation and delivers a more concentrated product. We can easily dry plant material at home using a food dehydrator. Just ensure you've thoroughly washed the plant material you want to use beforehand. When the dehydration process is finished, the plant material can be lightly ground and stored in a clean, airtight container. Protect dried plant material from sunlight and moisture.

There are four types of extracts commonly used in cosmetic preparation. The type of extract we use depends on the product we are creating. In this section, we'll take a look at how these extracts are prepared.

Glycolic Extract

This extract is prepared by mixing propylene glycol with vegetables. These extracts are useful for oil-based formulations. To prepare this extract, you'll need:

- An opaque, clean glass container.

- Died plant martial of your choice.

- Propylene glycol.

Directions:

Add dried plant material to the opaque, glass container. Pour enough propylene glycol to cover the plant material. Cover the mixture and store in a cool, dark, and dry place for two weeks. Remember to snake the container once a day for a better extract. After two weeks, filter the contents into a dark glass bottle and label for use.

Alcohol Extract/Tincture

Of all the solvents we can use to create extracts, alcohol is the one that extracts the most properties out of plants. Alcohol extracts can easily last between three and five years without losing their potency. To prepare the extract, you'll need to mix one part plant material with five parts alcohol. So if you use 10g of dried plant material, you'll need 50 ml of alcohol to create the extract. The materials you'll need are as follows:

- Clean, opaque glass container.

- Plant material of your choice (can use dried or fresh plant material).

- Alcohol.

Directions:

To the glass container add your chosen plant material. Cover the plant material with alcohol using the proportions indicated. Seal the container and store the mixture for two weeks in a dry, dark area. Protect the mixture from heat. Remember to shake the mixture daily to ensure better extraction. After two weeks, filter the contents into a dark glass bottle and label them for use.

Oleate/Infused Oil

These extracts are prepared by mixing mineral or vegetable oil with plant material. Olive, sunflower, and sweet almond oils are excellent base materials to create oleates with, adding significant amounts of vitamin E to our formulations. The added benefit is that vitamin E acts as a preservative, helping to keep the extract potent for longer. To prepare an infused oil, you'll need:

- Crushed and dried plant material.

- Opaque, glass container.

- Oil.

Directions:

Add crushed plant material to the opaque glass container. Cover the contents with oil and seal the container. Store the mixture for up to four weeks in a cool, dry, and dark place. Remember to shake the mixture daily to achieve full extraction of the plant material. After four weeks, filter the contents into a dark glass bottle and label for use.

Hydro-Glycerinated Extract

This extract is prepared by creating a mixture of 50% water and 50% glycerin. When the mixture is ready, use one part plant material to three parts of the prepared solvent. The mixture can be stored in the fridge to extend its shelf life from six months to a year. To prepare an extract of this kind, you'll need:

- Opaque glass container.

- Prepared solvent (equal parts water and glycerin).

- Dried plant material.

Directions:

Add the dried plant material to the glass container and top with solvent. Seal the container and store the mixture for 15 days in a cool, dark place away from moisture. Remember to shake the mixture daily to achieve full extraction of the contents. After 15 days, filter the continents into a dark glass bottle and label them for use.

Remember that not all types of extracts are suitable for all cosmetic products. The type of cosmetic product we are making will dictate the type of extract we'll use. For example, we can't use water-soluble extracts in massage oil, as the contents simply won't mix.

Glycolic, alcoholic, and hydro glycerinated extracts are perfect when formulations have a high percentage of water. Toners, gels, and shampoos are some of the products in which we'll use these extracts. If we are making massage oils, it is better to use oily extracts as they'll integrate much better with the base. Creams, serums, scrubs, and eye contours are the exception, and we can generally use any extract we like in these products.

Remember that adding more extract to a formulation does not guarantee a more impactful result or effective product. On the contrary, you could end up spoiling that cosmetic creation you've been working so hard on. So treat extracts the same as other ingredients: respectfully.

Beneficial Botanical Extracts and Ingredients

Botanical extracts are incredibly easy to make, but that does not mean all plant materials are equally beneficial for the skin. Some plants are very skin-loving, while others may leave us itching. The list of usable plant extracts for cosmetics can be quite extensive and intimidating in the beginning. For that reason, I've compiled a handy list of botanical extracts and useful ingredients that can be used in all your cosmetic creations.

- **Almond oil extract:** This ingredient helps to keep the skin hydrated by trapping moisture. Almond oil extract possesses soothing properties and is easily absorbed into the skin. It is an effective whitening ingredient and can help to reduce the appearance of stains. As an added bonus, all the vitamins present in the extract can help to delay the appearance of wrinkles.

- **Calendula extract:** This extract has moisturizing and soothing properties. Its powerful assets can retain water longer in the skin, so it is often used for dry, irritated, or sensitive skin. Another essential feature of calendula extract is that it has anti-inflammatory, antibacterial, and collagen regenerates; its soft power helps in preventing cases of tissue redness, rashes, or allergies.

- **Carrot extract:** Carrot extract is rich in carotenoids and vitamin E, two powerful oxidants that can prevent free radicals from gaining a foothold, thus protecting the skin from oxidation. In addition, it protects it from damage that the sun's rays can cause. Carrots also fat have ty acids, an effective emollient that helps moisturize, soften, and improve the skin's flexibility. The extract is ideal for formulating products that contain photoprotective anti-aging properties.

- **Chamomile extract:** In cosmetics, chamomile is used to cleanse, tone, soften and restore the balance of inflamed skin and decrease the appearance of open pores and marked veins that are especially seen near the eye area. Chamomile helps sensitive skin, irritated skin, and acne problems because it calms inflammation, especially if there is dermatitis or eczema in addition, its antiseptic and healing benefits make it an effective ally to heal and regenerate.

- **Cotton extract:** This extract is an excellent condition emollient. Thanks to its high content of unsaturated fatty acids, the extract tends to have a moisturizing and tightening effect. It is used in cosmetic products to improve the local circulation of the dermis, helping to revitalize it in the process. All those fatty acids present in cotton extracts also help to restore the lipid barrier of the skin.

- **Cucumber extract:** This ingredient helps balance the skin naturally due to its high content of vitamins and minerals, which help revitalize the skin, giving it a more luminous and fresh appearance. It has moisturizing and antioxidant properties, prevents water loss, and slows dehydration. In addition, part of its compounds form a protective film on the skin. It is ideal if you want a moisturizing, refreshing, decongestant, and softening effect in your products.

- **Lemon extract:** Lemon extract is rich in vitamin C, a powerful antioxidant that fights free radicals and photoaging, and is used to prevent the oxidation of tissues. Its acids stimulate cell regeneration by creating collagen and can reduce wrinkles and blemish skin due to the sun and aging. The flavonoids of the lemon extract are active and may help to improve overall circulation.

- **Oat extract:** Oatmeal is a cereal that contains omega-6 and omega-3, rich in fatty acids and essential for cell repair; it also has B vitamins, including folic acid and vitamin E. Oat extract is of high cleansing action because it absorbs all the dirt and residues that accumulate in the pores, the skin maintains its pH thanks to the proteins it contains. Remove dead skin cells and impurities such as pimples and other imperfections. Therefore, it helps to reduce the production of sebum and the formation of shine on the face.

- **Quinoa extract:** This moisturizing ingredient contains lysine, a critical element in synthesizing elastin and collagen, which tone the skin and prevent wrinkles and fine lines. Quinoa is a seed that has high levels of riboflavin; this means that it is rich in antioxidants, which provide the face with softness and elasticity and, in turn, contains vitamins C, E, and omega-6, which help restore the skin and reduce the grouping of melanin granules by attenuating dark spots and pigmentation—highly recommended for all skin types.

- **Sabila extract:** Aloe vera is a plant with healing properties, among which we can highlight as benefits for the skin. That is a natural astringent and anti-inflammatory that cleanses the face from its deepest layers, which favors the cleaning of pores and the elimination of impurities in the dermis. It is a moisturizer for the skin, regenerates tissue, stimulates and strengthens collagen and elastin fibers, and has antibacterial properties. Another property of aloe vera is healing; this renews increasing collagen formation and favors and Ing mated tissues' repair. It is recommended in products that seek to soften, moisturize, refresh, purify, and restore.

- **Rose petal extract:** Rose extract has antioxidant properties that moisturize and rejuvenate the skin, promote healing, and treat spots, stretch marks, and wrinkles. It has antioxidant benefits as it fights the oxidation of the skin, which is one of the leading causes of premature aging, blocking the action of free radicals and protecting the skin from external aggressions. On the other hand, it helps regulate excess oil in the skin, promotes tissue regeneration, and activates circulation. Highly recommended for use in anti-wrinkle products for mature skin or oily skin with acne problems.

- **Rosemary extract:** This extract is widely used to prepare hair, facial, and body products. It effectively fights free radicals that cause aging due to its antioxidant properties. Rosemary contains rosmarinic acid that has anti-inflammatory activities, making it ideal for soothing mild irritations in sensitive skin, and is also used if you need to improve the appearance of the skin and slow cellular aging.

Useful Active Ingredients

In addition to extracts, we can make use of active ingredients to make our cosmetic products truly superior. Some of the best active ingredients used by passionate cosmetics creators are listed below.

- **Caffeine:** Unlike the brew from the famous bean, the caffeine used in cosmetics is a solid, crystalline and white alkaloid. It is an excellent activator of blood circulation, fights free radicals, and reduces the appearance of wrinkles, sunspots, and loss of elasticity. The caffeine molecule is small, therefore, penetrates deep into the skin. It is one of the key ingredients in cosmetics to combat swelling, dull complexion, and skin oiliness, especially in the second chin and cheekbones. Caffeine helps eliminate or prevent bags that form under the eyes and tones the skin.

- **Collagen:** Collagen is our body's most abundant structural protein; it is part of all muscles and bones. Its function is to form fibers, from which the main structures of the organism are created; it works as a kind of glue that holds the tissues together, making them resistant and solid in appearance. As we age, collagen production decreases; this is noticeable because the skin becomes looser, wrinkles appear, and elasticity is lost. Its use in creams on the skin increases dehydration-prevented since it supports the dermis' fibers and increases firmness and resistance.

- **Elastin:** This protein works with collagen to improve the appearance of the skin. These proteins are closely related and never act independently of each other. They are present throughout the body, including joints, muscles, tissues, and bones. Elastin allows the skin to recover its normal state if it is stretched and returns to its original position instead of being flaccid or extended. Among its properties and benefits is having the ability to give a youthful and healthy appearance to the skin, allowing it to have young, youthful appearance keeps the skin hydrated, prevent breakage of connective tissue fibers, dermis, and epidermis, preventing ants the appearance of stretch marks, and slowing's facial aging.

- **Glycerin:** This colorless, odorless, antibacterial alcohol works as a cleaning agent. When applied, it stops the sticky sensation. Still, it should always be mixed with an oily substance because glycerin tends to absorb water and attract water, making the dermis retain it and resulting in hydrated and perfectly nourished skin. It stimulates our skin cells to rejuvenate them; tones soften them, and cleanses them. It is also ideal for treating cuts and burns and reduces inflammation and reactions to bites of various insects.

- **Hyaluronic acid:** Hyaluronic acid is a polysaccharide found on the inner surface of the cells of our body; it contains hydrophilic molecules which can absorb up to 1000 times their weight in water, which makes it an ally for the filling of wrinkles and expression lines by deeply hydrating them. Hyaluronic acid improves the appearance of the skin, giving it a younger appearance. I'll elaborate more on the usefulness of hyaluronic acid in the next chapter.

- **Lactic acid:** This ingredient increases the thickness of the dermis, achieving smoother and firmer skin, stimulating collagen production in the skin, making it more robust, and improving expressed fine lines and wrinkles. It purifies the skin as it cleanses the pore and is widely used in acne products and oily skin. It helps cell regeneration which helps eliminate spots on the face, redness, and others.

- **Vitamin E:** Vitamin E is an antioxidant, rejuvenating, and protective of free radicals that cause aging. Therefore, it prevents wrinkles, on the deterioration of skin tissue and works as a sunscreen. It works as a barrier and acts against inclement weather such as cold, heat, wind, and pollution. Regenerates and accelerates healing of skin tissues, is recommended for the lightening of scars once healed, and is also often used for postoperative wound treatments and deep exfoliations. Vitamin E is very effective in cleansing and toning the skin; it is also widely used in formulations to manufacture makeup removers.

Mastering the basics is essential to create high-quality cosmetic products. Now that you've seen how easily base products can be prepared, it is time to take your cosmetics education to the next level. In the next chapter, we'll take a closer look at products we can create to correct stains on the face.

·❤·❤·❤·❤·❤·

5

Products for Stained Faces

L atinas are truly a treasure trove of beauty tips and secrets. One way we can celebrate and perhaps preserve the advice our mothers, grand-mothers, and aunts shared is to incorporate them into cosmetic products. One challenge many from the latinas community face is stained skin. There are a number of reasons why the skin will stain, but prolonged UV and sun exposure tend to be the main culprit. To combat the scourge of stains on our faces, we often turn to depigmenting products. Those of us who use these products frequently may have noticed that depigmenting products have a lingua franca of their own. Descriptive words like brightening, fading, bleaching, or whitening are often used on the product label to describe the action. These products contain active ingredients that inhibit the production of melanin, lightening stains on the skin as a result.

Inhibiting the production of melanin is useful to reduce the appearance of facial stains and can prevent the appearance of new stains. Of course, we'll need to be careful about excessive sun exposure and wear sunscreen when we go outside. Changing hormones and aging are the other common reasons why stains may appear on the face. These products usually contain vitamin C, azelaic acid, serine, and other active ingredients. If you've mastered the basics in the previous chapter, whipping up the depigmenting products in this section should be fairly easy!

Before we explore different depigmenting products to create, keep the following usage guidelines in mind:

- A little goes a long way, so always try to apply the product evenly to the face. Depigmenting treatments should never be used as a spot treatment.

- Be patient and consistent with product use. The effects are usually noticeable from as early as six weeks. Allow the product to sit on your face for an hour before continuing with your regular skincare regimen.

- Use depigmenting creams and serums at night, this is when they are at their most effective.

- Always use sunscreen and be careful about over-using depigmenting products. If there is no noticeable improvement in the appearance of stains within eight weeks, it is best to consult a skincare professional.

Depigmenting Cream

This lightening product can be used to treat stains and encourages even skin tone. There are two stages to preparing this product, but it is relatively simple, and I'll walk you through it. The table below lists all the ingredients and the quantities you'll need if you are interested in small batches or large preparations. Always remember to work extremely accurately with your ingredients–a small attention to detail that greatly influences the result of the final product.

Materials	Quantity 100 ml	Quantity 1 liter
Base cream	65 gm	650 gm
Lactic Acid 30%	4 ml	40 ml
Kojic Acid 2%	4 ml	40 ml
Botanical extract (quinoa)	4 ml	40 ml
Preservative solution	4 ml	40 ml
Gel base	15 gm	150 gm
Fragrance (optional)	0,5 ml	5 ml
Vitamin E	3.5 ml	3.5 ml

Directions:

In the first stage, you'll need prepared base cream (the *Basic Cream Base* in the previous chapter is perfect). Measure the appropriate amount and add the botanical extract and vitamin E. Stir thoroughly to incorporate the ingredients. Next, we need to add preservatives, followed by lactic acid 30%. Mix the ingredients into the cream until you have a homogenous mixture. Stage one is now complete.

For stage two, we'll need to measure the appropriate amount of cosmetic gel base (the gel bases in chapter four can be used). Add kojic acid to the base and stir gently until combined with the gel base. If you are using any coloring or fragrance, now is the time to add these ingredients. Combine the gel base with the cream that we prepared in the first stage and mix until a homogenous mixture is formed. Stage two is now complete. Your depigmenting cream is now ready to be packaged, labeled, and used. Store the product in a clean, fresh, and dry environment.

$$\cdot \, \heartsuit \, \cdot \, \heartsuit \, \cdot \, \heartsuit \, \cdot \, \heartsuit \, \cdot \, \heartsuit \, \cdot$$

Depigmenting Cream From Scratch

If you don't have a prepared base cream ready, don't worry. This fairly simple depigmenting cream recipe will teach you how to create the product without using a base. Kojic acid is commonly used in brightening products, but it can be added to soap as well. The acid works by inhibiting melanin production. Over time, this reduces the appearance of dark spots and blemishes. As with all depigmenting products, it is best to use this cream at night. To make this depigmenting cream, you'll need:

Materials	Quantity 100 ml	Quantity 1 liter
Cetostearyl alcohol	32 ml	320 ml
Wheat germ oil	30 ml	300 ml
Propylene glycol	15 ml	150 ml
Polysorbate 20	15 ml	150 ml
Kojic acid	2 ml	20 ml
Preservative solution	4 ml	40 ml
Fragrance and colorants (optional)	S.Q. for desired	S.Q. for desired

Directions:

In a clean container, mix cetostearyl alcohol with wheat germ oil. This is the oily phase. In a separate container, start the aqueous phase by mixing demineralized water, polysorbate 20, and propylene glycol until homogeneous. Ready a water bath and place both containers in the bath. Heat the ingredients to 70ºC.

When the ingredients are at temperature, pour the demineralized water mixture into the wheat germ oil mixture. Be gentle as you do this, adding the liquid little by little to the oil while stirring vigorously to emulsify the mixture.

Powder the kojic acid (using a grinder or mortar and pestle) to a very fine consistency. Dilute the powdered kojic acid with some demineralized water (just a drop, don't use too much water) and add to the emulsified oil and water mixture. Add the preservative and optional ingredients. Test and adjust the pH if needed and store in an airtight container away from light, heat and moisture. A mini funnel can help to make bottling a bit easier. Don't forget to add a label with the date to your cosmetic creation.

$$\cdot\heartsuit\cdot\heartsuit\cdot\heartsuit\cdot\heartsuit\cdot\heartsuit\cdot$$

Depigmenting Toner

After cleansing the skin, it is advisable to use a toner that is suited for your skin type. Toners are wonderful products, removing impurities from the face and closing the pores. More importantly, toners help to maintain the pH of our skin. This depigmenting toner is gentle, yet effective. Incorporate the toner with the depigmenting cream featured above for the best stain-correcting results. The table below lists all the ingredients and quantities you'll need.

Materials	Quantity 100 ml	Quantity 1 liter
Aloe Vera Extract	2 ml	20 ml
Oat Extract	1 ml	10 ml
Fragrance (optional)	0,25 ml	2.5 ml
Preservative solution	4 ml	40 ml
Lactic acid 30%	3 ml	30 ml
Cosmetic Gel Base	20 gm	200 ml
Rose water	70 ml	700 ml

Directions:

In a clean, glass bowl, mix aloe vera, oat extract and cosmetic gel base until the ingredients are incorporated. Stir in the preservative solution. Now add the rose water little by little. The goal is to gently dilute the mixture to create a homogenous blend. Next, you'll need to add lactic acid and fragrance. Mix to form a homogenous fluid and store it in a suitable container with a label.

· ♥ · ♥ · ♥ · ♥ · ♥ ·

Depigmenting Vitamin C Serum

For luminous and clear skin, keep reading! This vitamin C serum is highly effective and super easy to make. It is recommended to keep this serum on hand if you are a smoker as it helps to stimulate collagen production, reducing some of the harmful effects smoking has on our skin (*Hacer serum vitamina C,* 2015). Vitamin C is a powerful ingredient and is used to treat skin problems caused by sun damage, spots, and acne. Skin tone should improve within three months of using this serum consistently. Keep in mind that this serum is highly photosensitive and should only be applied at night. Making this potent serum couldn't be easier, you'll need:

Materials	Quantity 100 ml	Quantity 1 liter
Vitamin C powder	5 gm	50 gm
Demineralized water	15 ml	150 ml
Liquid vegetable glycerin	80 ml	800 ml

Directions:

In a clean glass container, dissolve the vitamin C powder in demineralized water. Stir until the vitamin C is fully incorporated. Add vegetable glycerin and mix thoroughly to create an even blend. Store the serum in an amber dropper bottle away from light, heat, and moisture.

Moisturizing Protective Day Cream

The main reason why we use day creams is to keep the skin hydrated. This nourishing and protective day cream will help to keep the silky soft and beautifully hydrated, banishing those feelings of discomfort and tightness. Zinc oxide provides some protection from the sun and can help to maintain an even complexion with regular use. Carefully measure the ingredients shown in the table below, and you'll be well on your way to creating and enjoying this decadent face cream. Please note that this product is prepared in two stages.

Materials	Quantity 100 ml	Quantity 1 liter
Base cream	80 gm	800 gm
Botanical extract (cotton)	4 ml	40 ml
Titanium dioxide	1 gm	10 ml
Preservative solution	4 ml	40 ml
Zinc oxide	1 gm	10 ml
Fragance (optional)	0,5 ml	5 ml
Distilled water	10 ml	100 ml

Directions:

For the first stage, we'll need to mix titanium dioxide, zinc oxide, and water to form a homogeneous paste. That's the first stage complete. Set the paste aside for now and get to work on stage two of the preparation.

For the second stage, we need to take some prepared base cream and add botanical extracts and preservatives. Stir until the ingredients are incorporated. Now add the titanium dioxide and zinc oxide paste to the base cream. Add cosmetic coloring and fragrance if desired. Mix thoroughly to create a homogeneous blend and package in a suitable container with a label. Store in a clean, fresh, and dry environment.

· ♥ · ♥ · ♥ · ♥ · ♥ ·

Useful Acids in Cosmetic Products

Acids in cosmetic products are extremely versatile. In this section, you'll receive a crash course on various cosmetic acids and their use. The better we understand our ingredients and how to use them, the more effective our cosmetic creations will be. Acids are used to make creams, masks, serums, peels, and scrubs. Generally speaking, these ingredients help to exfoliate and cleanse the skin, giving it a renewed and smoother appearance. Of course, we must bear in mind that cosmetic acids, just like other cosmetic ingredients, need to be respected. Always follow manufacturer instructions and recommendations for the best results.

Another important thing to keep in mind is that the acids we use to formulate cosmetics should never come in direct contact with the skin. Too much of a good thing can be harmful. This is why we carefully measure cosmetic ingredients and enjoy their benefits by mixing them with a base product or incorporating them into formulations. Furthermore, cosmetics that contain acids are best used at night, as some of these ingredients are photosensitive. Always use good sunscreen to help reduce and prevent the appearance of blemishes and sun damage.

There is a minor restriction on the use of cosmetic acids (especially the ones I'll discuss in this section). They should never be used with carbopol gel bases (*Ácidos en cosmética: ¡Descubre el mejor para tu piel!*, 2020). That's because cosmetic acids can and will normally liquefy the carbopol gel bases completely, leaving us with an unusable waste of ingredients. Now, with those basics out of the way, let's learn more about cosmetic acids!

Hyaluronic Acid: A Deeply Moisturizing and Anti-aging Powerhouse

The average person is likely to be familiar with the name of this skin-loving ingredient, most likely through marketing campaigns driven by big, well-known skincare brands. But what exactly is hyaluronic acid, and why is the cosmetics industry so in love with this ingredient? When I explain the science behind it all, you'll likely fall in love with the ingredient, too!

Hyaluronic acid is found widely throughout the human body. It can be found in connective tissues as well as epithelial and neural tissues. Hyaluronic acid has unique characteristics, and researchers wanted to know how much of it is present in the human body. They found that an average person, weighing 70 kg, had roughly 15g of hyaluronic acid in their bodies (Stern, 2004). The same study determined that of this supply, roughly 5g (or one-third) will be used daily. A major component of the extracellular matrix, hyaluronic acid plays an important role in healthy cell functioning.

Excessive exposure to UV rays damages skin cells to the extent that they don't produce as much hyaluronic acid as before (*Hyaluronic Acid,* 2019). This is why skincare professionals will always encourage the use of sunscreen. Since hyaluronic acid plays a big role in our skin's natural repair processes, our skin's degradation is sped up when these cells produce less of it. All of this translates into an older appearance. Cosmetic products continuing hyaluronic acid give the skin's repair processes a little boost, often with impressive results. Hyaluronic acid molecules can capture up to 1000 times its own weight in water, which explains their deeply moisturizing effect.

Hyaluronic acid is available as a fluid or powder. We'll need to dissolve the powder before incorporating it into formulations. The regenerative properties of this ingredient make it especially valuable for mature skin (older than 35), preventing dehydration, filling in expression lines and wrinkles, and encouraging the production of collagen. The result? Skin with a smoother, firmer, and tighter appearance. It is a powerful, skin-loving ingredient that certainly deserves the love it is receiving!

Glycolic Acid: Cell Renewal and Stain Reduction

Skin types that are prone to developing acne and blemishes will benefit from this acid. Glycolic acid also helps to improve the appearance of wrinkles as it encourages cell renewal. The ingredient is also known to have an exfoliation action, cleaning the pores and ridding the skin of dead cells. Cleaner skin absorbs active ingredients better, improving its effectiveness.

Glycolic acid is useful to fade stains. It is often used to fade spots and acne scars and encourages collagen production. In short, glycolic acid leaves us with clear and luminous skin. That being said, it is a photosensitive ingredient and should only be used in cosmetic formulations designed to be used at night.

Ascorbic Acid: An Antioxidant for Luminous Skin

Vitamin C is very popular in cosmetic products and for good reason! It is a powerful antioxidant, making it useful in the fight against wrinkles and expression lines. By reducing the damage free radicals cause to our skin, ascorbic acid helps to preserve firmness and elasticity. The vitamin gives the skin a luminous glow and encourages collagen production. This ingredient is essential in natural cosmetics.

Ascorbic acid can be combined with vitamin E to gently and effectively fade blemishes. Keep in mind that vitamin C is photosensitive, so it is best to use this ingredient in products that are intended for nighttime usage. Formulations containing vitamin C are sensitive to heat and should be kept in a cool place, away from direct light.

Salicylic Acid: Our Ally Against Acne

Salicylic acid is commonly used in products formulated to treat acne. The ingredient has good antibacterial and exfoliating properties, making it useful to keep pores clear. Be careful of overuse as it can lead to irritation and sensitivity. Salicylic acid acts as a mild peeling agent (keratolytic agent) and helps to stimulate cell renewal. The ingredient can be used in creams, serums, soaps, facial cleansers, and masks. The dose can vary between 0.5% and 2% of the total formula weight.

Kojic Acid: Unifies Skin Tone

This cosmetic acid inhibits melanin production, making it a key ingredient in depigmenting products. To create kojic acid, manufacturers will use a specific fermentation process that involves rice and fungi. This results in a gentle, but effective ingredient that can help to even skin tone. It is effective against blemishes caused by sun exposure, hormonal imbalances, and the aging process. Kojic acid is rich in antioxidants and leaves the skin feeling softer. When using kojic acid, be very precise when weighing. The dose typically used should not exceed one percent of the total weight of the formulation used.

Creating cosmetics to combat uneven skin tone and blemishes is surprisingly easy. Be extra careful with your measurements when preparing these products. Cosmetic acids are incredibly powerful ingredients and can irritate the skin if used in incorrect dosages. When labeling depigmenting products for sale, be sure to include usage instructions, as some of the ingredients are photosensitive. Blemishes are only one challenge Latinx skin faces. In the next chapter, I'll guide you on how to create gentle and effective products for oily skin.

· ❤ · ❤ · ❤ · ❤ · ❤ ·

6

Products for Oily Skin

One of the biggest mistakes we can make in caring for our skin is over-cleansing, especially oily skin types. Over-cleansing strips the skin of beneficial oils, triggering the sebaceous glands to produce more sebum. This secretion helps to lubricate the skin and hair, but sebum also plays a vital role in keeping the skin's protective acid mantle intact (Kunin, n.d.). Oily skin presents a unique challenge, making it tricky to manage. On the one hand, a mattified appearance is desirable. Anyone who has experienced the discomfort of excessively oily skin knows firsthand how this can impact our self-esteem and confidence in public spaces. On the other hand, we don't want to over-strip the skin and cause harm to the acid mantle. This is why skincare professionals will always recommend gel skincare products. These formulations are gentle enough to remove excess oil without stripping the skin bare–formulations that I'll teach you in this chapter. Before we leap head-long into the fun part, it is necessary to understand a few things about oily skin:

- **Genetics plays a role:** If one of your parents has oily skin, it is likely you'll develop oily skin too, since it is a familial trait (Leiva,

2019).

- **Hormonal fluctuations can cause oily skin:** Whether we are going through puberty, menopause, or stressful times, changes in our hormones can trigger the production of excess sebum. Androgens are the culprit behind this most of the time, as they signal sebaceous glands to produce more oil.

- **Using the wrong skincare products leads to oily skin:** Cosmetic gels and water-based products are always recommended for oily skin because they don't introduce additional oils and fats to the skin. What oily skin needs most is to remain hydrated. This makes gels and water-based products the ideal vehicle to deliver active ingredients to the skin.

- **Oil blotting papers won't aggravate oily skin:** They are a saving grace for many who have excessively oily skin and helps us maintain a matte appearance throughout the day. Blotting papers are designed to absorb excess oil and won't irritate the skin when used correctly. When using blotting papers, you only need to follow one rule: Use the paper dab, never rub it over the skin.

A common sign of oily skin includes noticing that your face is shiny an hour or two after cleansing. Other signs include: Makeup generally does have staying power through the day. Visible blackheads, acne flare-ups, and large pores can be observed and the skin feels greasy to the touch. There's no denying that oily skin can be a challenge to manage, but I'll share some tips that will help us get the most out of our cosmetic creations.

- Avoid excessive cleansing with harsh scrubs. Over-exfoliating only signals the skin to produce more oil.

- Steer clear from emollients. We need to prevent dehydration in oily skin types, making cosmetic gels, and water-based products the best medium for the job.

- Avoid using bar soaps on the face. This is true for all skin types, not just oily skin. Bar soaps are filled with harsh surfactants that can strip all the beneficial oils from the skin.

- Don't skip the toner! This important step helps to balance the skin's pH, helping to keep the skin hydrated (Steadman, 2017).

$\cdot \heartsuit \cdot \heartsuit \cdot \heartsuit \cdot \heartsuit \cdot \heartsuit \cdot$

Moisturizing Daytime Gel for Oily Skin

Oily skin can become dehydrated, so we need to pay attention to our daily hydration. Daily hydration is one of the primary and most important skin care steps we can take to maintain young, healthy, and radiant skin. External factors may impact the moisture content in our skin, often dehydrating it. This holds true for all skin types.

Moisturizing gels are recommended for use on the face to deliver water and antioxidants to skin cells. We don't have to be too concerned with emollients when making products for oily skin types. Gel formulations are light in texture and easily absorbed as the main ingredient is water made up of small molecules of moraine oil. There's a good reason for selecting this type of product, as it allows us to slightly increase the concentrations of certain non-acidic ingredients. This is necessary to nourish the face through adequate hydration without introducing excess fat. The table below details the ingredients you'll need to make this intensely hydrating and nourishing base gel.

Important note: Extracts recommended for use in cosmetic products for oily skin: Chamomile, cucumber, and organic rice. Apply the gel after cleansing the face. Gently massage the product in and complete the routine with sunscreen for best results.

Materials	Quantity 100 ml	Quantity 1 liter
Quinoa extract	5 ml	50 ml
Oat extract	5 ml	50 ml
Preservative solution	5 ml	50 ml
Cosmetic base gel	65 gm	650 gm
Distilled water	20 ml	200 ml
Fragrance (optional)	0,2 - 0,5 ml	2 - 5 ml

Directions:

Add the distilled water to the cosmetic gel base (the gel base from Chapter 4 is recommended). Pour the distilled water little by little into the gel base. The goal is to hydrate the gel as we slowly mix the two ingredients. After this, we can add the preservative solution and extracts. If you are using cosmetic colorants and fragrances, they can be added at this stage. Mix to form a homogenous product and test the pH. The acidity should be between 5.9 and 6.1, so adjust it if needed. Store the product in a suitable container and label it with the production date. Store in a cool, dry place and keep the gel away from direct light.

·♥ · ♥ · ♥ · ♥ · ♥·

Revitalizing Serum for Oily Skin

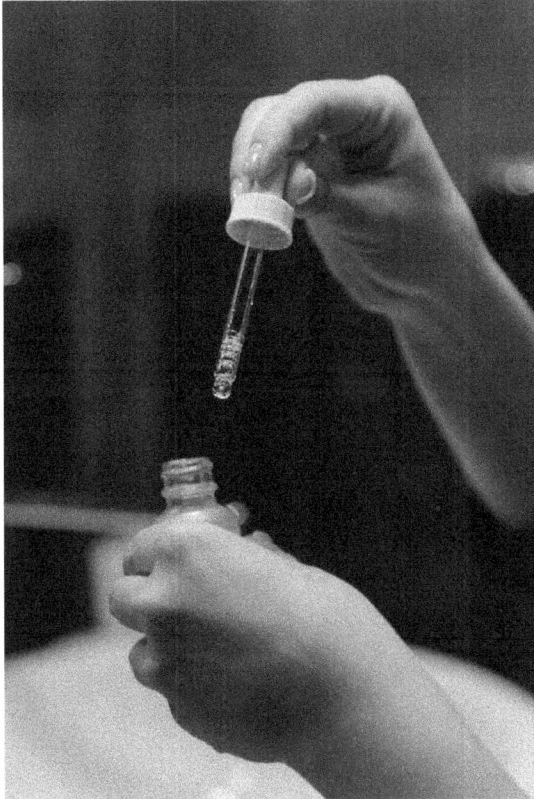

This light and deeply moisturizing formulation will leave the skin feeling soft and supple without sticky residue. The table below details the ingredients and quantities needed.

Materials	Quantity 100 ml	Quantity 1 liter
Xanthan gum	1 gm	10 gm
Lactic Acid 20%	3 ml	20 ml
Preservative solution	4 ml	40 ml
Hyaluronic acid	2 ml	20 ml
Distilled water	90 ml	900 ml
Fragrance (optional)	0,2 ml	2 ml

Directions:

In a clean, glass bowl, hydrate the Xanthan gum by adding distilled water little by little. Stir slowly as you add the distilled water to fully hydrate the gum. Next, we need to add the preservative, followed by hyaluronic and lactic acids. All these acids one at a time into the mixture, stirring the gum gently to fully incorporate the ingredients. When the acids are completely blended into the product, we can add fragrance if desired. From here, the product goes into a suitable container with a label. Store the serum in a clean, fresh and dry environment.

· ♥ · ♥ · ♥ · ♥ · ♥ ·

Cleansing Gel for Oily Skin

One of the secrets to beautiful, healthy skin is daily cleansing. Gentle cleansing gels are among the best products for oily skin. These products gently remove impurities and excess oil and effectively deliver active ingredients to the skin, leaving it luminous. I'll share how to create this product, however, it is necessary to elaborate on the active ingredients used:

- **Coconut betaine:** An ingredient with surfactant properties and a near-perfect pH. The pH usually ranges between five and six, making it highly compatible with our skin. Coconut betaine has gentle cleansing properties and is often used in products designed for sensitive skin and baby products. The ingredient exerts a slight antibacterial effect.

- **Quinoa extract:** A powerful moisturizer rich in lysine, useful to prevent wrinkles and tone the skin. Quinoa is rich in antioxidants, which give the face softness and improve skin elasticity. The ingredient has restorative properties and can help to reduce the appearance of blemishes.

- **Aloe vera:** This plant is well-known for its healing properties and is a skin-loving ingredient. The natural astringent properties of aloe vera cleanse the skin, unclogs pores, and eliminates impurities. Aloe vera gives us all of this cleansing action without drying the skin. Its antibacterial properties also help to ensure that the skin remains clearer for longer.

Materials	*Quantity 100 ml*	*Quantity 1 liter*
Liquid Soap Base	60 ml	600 ml
Acetyl dimethyl ammonium chloride (Dehyquart)	1 ml	10 ml
Preservative solution	4 ml	40 ml
Sodium chloride (Thickener)	S.Q. for desired thickness	S.Q. for desired thickness
Diethanolamide (coconut betaine)	5 ml	50 ml
Distilled water	30 ml	300 ml

Directions:

Pour distilled water into a clean container and add the liquid soap base little by little. Stir gently to blend the ingredients. Feel free to use the soap base mentioned in Chapter 4 to create this product. Next, we need to add the preservative solution followed by the dehyquart. Stir to fully incorporate the ingredients and adjust the viscosity of the product with sodium chloride. Finally, measure and adjust the pH and store the product in a suitable container with a label and production date. It is best to use this product on damp skin. Massage the skin lightly to create foam and then rinse to reveal beautifully clean skin.

· ♥ · ♥ · ♥ · ♥ · ♥ ·

Dermoprotective Facial Soap

For those who don't like gel cleansers, this gentle soap formulation might be worth looking at. The end product is suitable for sensitive skin and is made from easy-to-find ingredients. The main ingredient is a soap base. The soap base covered in Chapter 4 is ideal, but feel free to use a different soap base if desired. The soap base you use should be gentle on the skin and neutral. Oat and chamomile extracts are used to firm and soften the skin (*How to Make Homemade Soap for the Face*, 2016). These ingredients are useful to help eliminate blemishes and inflammation, leaving the skin deeply moisturized. When adding a scent to this kind of soap, it is best to use a hydrosol or floral water filled with skin-loving benefits. Rose hydrosol generally fits the bill as it has anti-inflammatory, astringent, and refreshing properties. To make 200 CC of this liquid facial soap, you'll need:

Materials	Quantity 100 CC	Quantity 1 liter
Prepared soap base	90 CC	900 ml
Chamomile extract	4 CC	40 ml
Oat extract	4 CC	40 ml
Rose hydrosol	6 drops	12 drops
Cosmetic grade coloring (optional)	S.Q. for desired	S.Q. for desired

Directions:

Measure the desired amount of soap base and gently stir chamomile and oat extracts in. Add the extracts one at a time, little by little, as you stir gently. Stir well to fully incorporate the ingredients. Next, we add rose hydrosol and cosmetic grade colorant if desired and stir until a homogeneous mixture is created. Transfer the product to a suitable container and label with the production date.

Oily skin can be improved with proper skincare routines and a healthy diet. Making our own skincare products is a great way of ensuring we don't introduce any unwanted ingredients to the skin. In the next chapter, we'll take a closer look at anti-aging products.

♥ • ♥ • ♥ • ♥ • ♥

7

Anti-Aging Products

How we all wish that our skin can remain spotless and youthful! Just because you are sporting a few wrinkles and fine lines does not mean your hopes of achieving a younger, more radiant appearance are dashed. Just a glance in the cosmetics aisle of your favorite store is enough to see that there is no shortage of anti-aging products available. Some work, while others may have interesting but unwanted side effects. Not to mention the price tag on some brands! What is a person to do?

We know that the battle against wrinkles and fine lines is a constant one, but with the right skincare routine, it does not have to be a slog. If you are in your 30s, it is advisable to keep the formulations of the anti-aging products discussed in this chapter close at hand. Your skin will thank you for it! These DIY anti-aging products are fun to make and tend to be cheaper and more effective than most products available on the market.

· ♥ · ♥ · ♥ · ♥ · ♥ ·

Biphasic Makeup Remover

Our eyes and lips are two of the most sensitive parts on the face. The skin is at its thinnest in these areas, so we need to be careful. Especially when removing makeup. The solution? A biphasic makeup remover. The gentle formulation easily targets and removes greasy components of makeup and pigments, leaving the skin feeling soft and ready for a deep cleanse. The table below details all the ingredients and quantities you'll need to create this product:

Material	Quantity 100 ml	Quantity 1 liter
Mineral oil	35 ml	350 ml
Almond oil	5 ml	50 ml
Distilled water	25 ml	250 ml
Sabila extract	5 ml	50 ml
Silicone 245	20 ml	200 ml
Oil-soluble coloring (optional)	S.Q. for desired	S.Q. for desired
Water-soluble dye (optional)	S.Q. for desired	S.Q. for desired
Fragrance	0,25 ml	2,5 ml
Preservative solution	4 ml	40 ml
Isopropyl myristate	6 ml	60 ml

Directions:

Start the oil phase by mixing Isopropyl Myristate with the fragrance. Gradually incorporate the mineral oil into this mixture. Silicone to the mixture and stir thoroughly. You can add oil-soluble colorants to the mixture if desired. Next, we need to start the aqueous phase by mixing distilled water, water solution colorant (optional), and the preservative solution together. Incorporate the liquid into the oil phase little by little and constantly stir to create a homogenous product. Once all the liquid has been successfully blended into the oil mixture, the product can be stored in a suitable container and labeled. To use, simply mix the two phases and use a cotton ball or disc to gently remove makeup. Wash the face with a cleansing gel afterward.

· ❤ · ❤ · ❤ · ❤ · ❤ ·

Cleansing Milk

Cleansing milk is helpful to keep our face clean and sanitized daily, freeing the skin from traces of makeup, dead cells, sweat, and impurities. This formulation goes the extra mile by providing adequate hydration and toning of the face. To make this gentle formulation, inspect the ingredients and quantities in the table below.

Materials	Quantity 100 ml	Quantity 1 liter
Base cream	40 gm	400 gm
Texapon 70	1 ml	10 ml
Tween 20	2 ml	20 ml
Aloe vera extract	1 ml	10 ml
Quinoa extract	2 ml	20 ml
Water-soluble dye (optional)	S.Q. for desired	S.Q. for desired
Fragrance (optional)	0,5 ml	5 ml
Preservative solution	4 ml	40 ml
Distilled water	50 ml	50 ml

Directions:

Start the aqueous phase by heating the weather to 70 °C. Remove it from the heat once the temperature has been reached. Add Texapon 70 and Tween 20 to the water and mix well. Now we need to add the mixture to the base cream and blend until an even emulsion forms. Continue to beat the mixture until it has cooled, gradually adding the extract, preservative, and fragrance to the product. Store the product in a suitable container and label it with the date of production. Don't forget to include usage instructions on the label. To use, spread the cleansing milk evenly over the face using the fingertips. Massage the product into the skin for a few seconds. Remove using a cotton pad or damp sponge and rinse the skin.

· ♥ · ♥ · ♥ · ♥ · ♥ ·

Nourishing Anti-Wrinkle Repair Cream

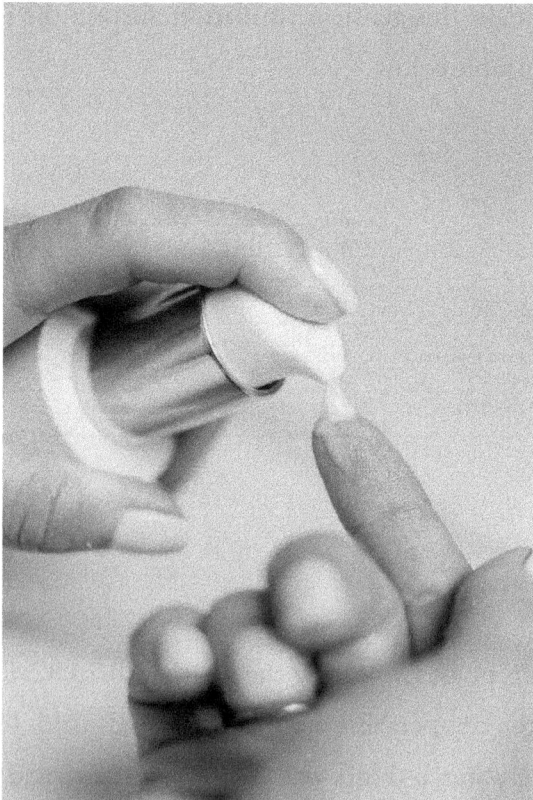

When night comes, the body prepares to rest and recover from all the activity carried out during the day, that's why skincare professionals will always recommend the use of a repair cream or serum at night. After all, what is used on the face at that time gains tremendous importance. The body is programmed to regenerate at night and absorb nutrients more easily during rest; hence, nourishing creams are recommended for use at night. This type of cream is more unctuous than day creams, so I recommend steering clear of it if you are under 30 years of age or have skin that is prone to developing acne. That being said, this nourishing cream is a rich emulsion that lubricates, softens, and encourages cell renewal and repair. It is a powerful regenerating cream. I've listed the ingredients in the table below.

Materials	*Quantity 100 ml*	*Quantity 1 lit*
Base cream	85 gm	850 gm
Botanical extract	3 ml	30 ml
Vegetable oil (olive)	2 ml	20 ml
Vegetable oil (almond)	2 ml	20 ml
Preservative solution	4 ml	40 ml
Water-soluble cosmetic coloring (optional)	S.Q. for desired	S.Q. for desired
Fragrance (optional)	0,5 ml	5 ml
Hyaluronic acid	1 ml	10 ml
Collagen	1 ml	10 ml
Elastin	0,5 ml	5 ml
Vitamin E	1 ml	10 ml

Directions:

Take the base cream and slowly add the botanical extract. Stir continuously to ensure an even blend. Next, we need to add the natural oils and preservatives. Add these ingredients one by one as you continuously stir. Add the cosmetic coloring and fragrance if desired. Continue to mix as you add hyaluronic acid, collagen, elastin, and vitamin E. Check and adjust the pH if needed. The pH needs to be between 4.9 and 5.1. Package the product in a suitable container and label it with the production date and usage instructions. To use, apply the product every night after the face has been cleansed with a cleansing gel. Apply on the eye contour and neck as and work the product in with a gentle massage.

Anti-aging products form a vital part of skin care in our 30s and onwards. While they may contain more ingredients than most formulations listed in this book, learning how to make anti-aging cosmetic products can be useful in two ways. First, it allows us to expand the product line we can offer to potential clients. Anti-aging creams and serums are popular products, so expanding a potential product line this way makes sense. Secondly, anti-aging products are notoriously expensive. When we learn how to make these products ourselves, it is much easier to benefit from freshly prepared formulations. Believe me, there is a difference in the efficacy of a product that's been newly prepared versus one that's been sitting on a retail shelf somewhere. Speaking of effective skincare solutions, in the next chapter, we'll take a look at the products we can make to take care of sensitive skin types.

· ❤ · ❤ · ❤ · ❤ · ❤ ·

8

Products for Sensitive Skin

"**S**ensitive skin" is a term that we use a lot in the skincare world. The phrase is used to refer to skin that is easily irritated. The sun, wind, temperature, and some topical products can all contribute to the skin's reactivity, causing the skin to become red and itchy. In this light, "sensitive skin" is more of a blanket term than a medical expression, which necessitates that we keep the following things in mind when creating products for this skin type.

- **Ongoing Sensitivity May Indicate an Underlying Condition:** Anyone's skin can react to the ingredients used in cosmetic products. These reactions are usually brief and easy to avoid once we've pinned down the cause. However, ongoing sensitivity can be a sign that you might be dealing with eczema, rosacea, psoriasis, contact dermatitis, or other underlying issues (Nast, 2018). It is best to seek the help of a skincare professional if you are experiencing ongoing sensitivity.

- **Skin sensitivity is tied with the lipid barrier:** The lipid barrier is responsible to keep moisture in the skin whilst shielding it from potentially damaging things (harsh chemicals, UV rays, etc.). When the lipid barrier is compromised, it becomes easier for irritants to penetrate the barrier and inflame our skin.

- **It is common for aging skin to become more sensitive:** The lipid barrier tends to break down as we age, leading to increased skin sensitivity over time. That's because the lipid barrier does not replace itself as frequently as we grow older. This leads to the lipid barrier being compromised, which explains why products we've been using without problem for years suddenly irritate the skin.

- **Unscented and fragrance-free are not synonyms:** At least when it comes to cosmetic products, the two terms are not interchangeable. Fragrance-free products are exactly that, products that do not contain any fragrance. You'll notice that the use of cosmetic coloring and fragrance is optional in most cosmetic formulations, and there's a good reason for this. Fragrance is frequently the culprit that triggers sensitive skin. "Unscented" products may still contain fragrances and other ingredients to create a neutral smell and are not considered fragrance-free products.

Those with sensitive skin are encouraged to perform a patch test before adding new products to their routine. To perform the patch test, simply take a small amount of product and apply it to the delicate skin by your wrist. Observe the application site for a few hours. If no reaction occurs, the product can be safely added to your routine. That being said, it is best to keep the skincare routine simple. A gentle cleansing foam, soothing toner, and moisturizer are all you'll need in most cases. These products are super gentle on the skin and relatively easy to make. Just take a look!

· ❤ · ❤ · ❤ · ❤ · ❤ ·

Cleansing Foam

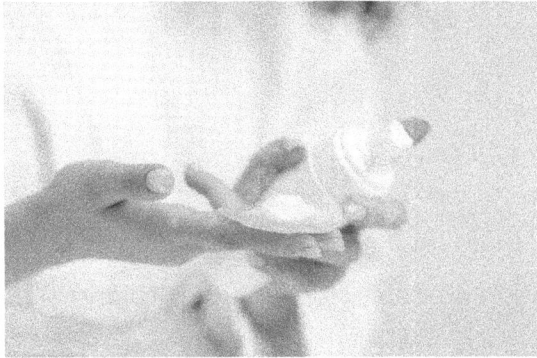

Cleansing foam is a product that is easy to comprehend. It's a cleanser with high foaming potential, turning sudsy as it is lathered on the face. The foam is gentle and lifts dirt and impurities from the skin and pores, leaving the skin feeling and looking fresher. To make this formulation, carefully measure the ingredients detailed in the table below:

Materials	Quantity 100 ml	Quantity 1 liter
Quinoa extract	2 ml	20 ml
Oat extract	2 ml	20 ml
Liquid vegetable glycerin	6 ml	60 ml
Preservative solution	5 ml	50 ml
Cocamidopropyl betaine	10 ml	100 ml
Distilled water	75 ml	750 ml

Directions:

Pour the Cocamidopropyl betaine into the water and stir slowly, so it does not make much foam. Now gently add the vegetable glycerin, extracts, and preservative. Continue to mix the mixture until all the ingredients are well incorporated. Package in a suitable container (preferably one with a dosing pump) and label with the date of production.

· ❤ · ❤ · ❤ · ❤ · ❤ ·

Moisturizer for Sensitive Skin

This product helps to strengthen the skin and improves elasticity and the appearance of expression lines for a rejuvenated appearance. In sensitive skin, dehydration can cause irritation, which often generates pain, sensitivity, and itchiness. That's because the protective barrier of this skin may be weak. Using this moisturizer, we help the skin strengthen the lipid barrier and recover moisture levels to make it stronger and more resistant to external pollutants, exposure to low temperatures, and dry air.

With daily use of the moisturizer, it is guaranteed to improve the appearance of your skin visibly. You'll be able to enjoy a luminous complexion as the product penetrates deeply into the skin, improving elasticity while delivering much-needed hydration to the face. To make this skin-loving cream, carefully measure the ingredients in the table below and follow the directions.

Materials	Quantity 100 ml	Quantity 1 liter
Base cream	85 gm	850 gm
Botanical extract (cotton)	4 ml	40 ml
Botanical extract (quinoa)	4 ml	40 ml
Preservative solution	4 ml	40 ml
Water-soluble cosmetic coloring (optional)	S.Q. for desired	S.Q. for desired
Fragrance (optional)	0,5 ml	5 ml
Vitamin E	2.5 ml	25 ml

Directions:

Weight the base cream carefully. Add the botanical extracts to the cream while constantly stirring. Add the extracts one at a time. Stir the preservative in and add the optional ingredients if desired (coloring and fragrance). Add vitamin E and stir to form a homogeneous blend. Test and adjust the pH, it should have an acidity of between 4.9 and 5.1. After the pH has been adjusted, store the product in a suitable container and label it with the production date. Store in a cool, fresh, and dry environment. To use the product, simply apply it to the face with a gentle massage after using a cleansing gel and decongestant toner. To complement the daily routine, use a nourishing cream at night.

·❤ · ❤ · ❤ · ❤ · ❤ ·

Soothing Toner for Sensitive Skin

Daily facial cleansing can leave the pores irritated and dilated. This facial toner helps to decongest and refresh the skin, restoring its softness and luminosity. It also helps improve blood circulation and promote cell regeneration, giving a feeling of firmness and elasticity for its emollient effect, protecting the skin from daily fatigue. To create this product, follow the ingredients, measurements, and directions stated below.

Important note: Recommended extracts for dry skin include carrots and non-citrus fruits. Chamomile, cucumber, and organic rice extracts are best for oily skin.

Materials	Quantity 100 ml	Quantity 1 liter
Quinoa extract	1 ml	10 ml
Oat extract	1 ml	10 ml
Chamomile extract	3 ml	30 ml
Preservative solution	5 ml	50 ml
Propilenglicol	10 ml	100 ml
Distilled water	80 ml	800 ml

Directions:

In a clean, glass mixing bowl, combine quinoa, oat extract, and chamomile extract. Keep stirring as you add the preservative solution next. Stir until the ingredients are fully blended. Next, add distilled water in small amounts at a time as you continuously stir. Follow this up with Propilenglicol and mix to form a homogeneous liquid. Store in a suitable container (preferably with a spray cap) and label with the production date. Remember to cleanse the face before applying the toner. For easy application, simply spray the toner on the face and allow it to dry naturally. Use it in the morning, evenings, or during the day to refresh the skin.

Regular care with gentle products can make a dramatic difference to sensitive skin. The products discussed in this chapter are designed to soothe sensitive skin, leaving it supple and radiant. To bring the best out of our skin, we need to use products designed for our skin type and the problems we want to address. One problem that can sneak up unsuspectingly is dark circles, but we'll take a closer look at products to treat them in the next chapter.

· ♥ · ♥ · ♥ · ♥ · ♥ ·

9
Products for Dark Circles

Many women struggle with idiopathic orbital ring hypochromia (dark circles). These marks can appear under the eyes even when the best skincare regimen is followed religiously. Most of the time, we assume dark circles are caused by a lack of sleep, but it is not that simple. There are many things that contribute to the formation of dark circles such as tiredness, aging, allergies, changing hormones, malnutrition, smoking, circulation problems, and inadequate sun protection. The wide scope of causes makes dark circles a fairly common problem, one that is compounded by the fact that our eye contour generally has low levels of collagen. This allows fluids and toxins to build up under the skin, resulting in that raccoon-eyed appearance we all know and loathe. While dark circles and bags under the eyes often occur together, the two are not the same. Dark circles specifically relate to an increase in pigmentation in the eye area. The color of dark circles usually gives us a clue as to what the possible cause may be. Let's take a closer look.

- **Transient dark circles**

These types of dark circles have a distinctive blue color. They are fairly easy to recognize and treat. The main cause is fatigue. Healthy lifestyle choices and ensuring you get enough quality sleep will go a long way to keep those blue splotches under control. If you are working remotely and staring at a computer screen for most of the day, remember to take regular 20-minute breaks. This helps to rest the eyes, reducing the appearance of transient dark circles. Iron deficiency is often linked with dark circles, so ensuring that your diet contains enough iron is another preventative step that can be taken. If transient dark circles are accompanied by bags under the eyes, it may be necessary to adjust your salt intake.

- **Hyperpigmented dark circles**

These dark circles are brown in color. They are caused by increased melanin production in the area. The bad news is that hyperpigmented dark circles are usually genetic in origin, and they are the most difficult to treat. Treatment options are available and well-trained professionals will be able to point you in the right direction. Topical treatments for hyperpigmented dark circles usually focus on keeping the skin hydrated and providing some firmness to the eye contour.

- **Sunken dark circles**

These marks are also called furrows. They appear when we experience fat loss in the eye area and run from the inner corner of the eye to the cheek. These dark circles mainly appear due to aging, health issues, dehydration, or vitamin deficiencies.

- **Vascular dark circles**

Purple or dark blue in color, these dark circles are mainly caused by the dilation of blood vessels and the thinning of our skin in the eye area. Allergies are often the trigger. When the body reacts to an allergy, histamines are released in the bloodstream, which dilates blood vessels (Watson, 2020). The dilated blood vessels become more visible beneath the skin and show up as purple or dark blue marks beneath our eyes. In a pinch, a cold compress with black tea or green tea will help to shrink dilated blood vessels, reducing the appearance of puffy eyes.

Prevention of Dark Circles

The old adage "prevention is better than the cure" certainly seems to ring true here. Our eyes accentuate our natural beauty and unsightly dark circles and strip the face from that youthful, radiant appearance. When we wake up to dark circles, a normal reaction would be to reach for the makeup kit to hide the appearance thereof. Doing so only masks the problem and does not address it. Besides, daily makeup usage comes with a drawback as it can encourage the deterioration process to speed up when it is not removed properly. A few simple lifestyle adjustments can go a long way to prevent most dark circles from forming. However, some dark circles may persist even after reversible factors are addressed. For these cases, it is best to rely on the expertise of a skincare professional. Broadly speaking, the lifestyle adjustments needed to prevent most dark circles are:

- **Wearing sunglasses:** Sunglasses that have quality UVA and UVB filters are the best to protect the delicate eye area from those harsh rays. Don't forget to use sunscreen before going outside.

- **Sleep enough:** Most adults need around nine hours of sleep every night. Having a bedtime routine can help improve the quality of our sleep, especially when we avoid using mobile devices in bed.

- **Healthy diet:** When we eat a healthy, balanced diet, our skin is radiantly happy. Ensure your diet contains enough vitamins C and K as well as zinc and iron. These nutrients will help to prevent the appearance of dark circles related to poor nutrition.

- **Go easy on caffeine:** Excessive caffeine consumption can lead to restlessness and trouble sleeping, which encourages dark circles to appear. Cutting back on caffeinated beverages helps us rest better, thus reducing the appearance of very preventable dark circles.

- **Don't neglect hydration:** Our bodies need adequate hydration to function properly, especially when it comes to blood circulation. Problems with circulation usually show up in the blood vessels, manifesting as dark circles beneath the eyes. Avoiding dehydration is one of the easiest steps we can take to prevent dark circles whilst giving our skin and bodies a boost.

- **Eye contour helps:** These products are specially formulated to treat the sensitive area around the eye without causing irritation. Using any moisturizer in the eye area can promote premature aging and will do nothing for dark circles. To effectively treat dark circles, it is best to use an eye contour that deeply nourishes the skin while treating irregular pigmentation.

- **Get the heart pumping:** Regular exercise is important to keep our circulatory system in good working order and helps with the elimination of fluid retention. Exercise is also a great way to get rid of stress and pent-up energy that may be interfering with a good night's rest.

- **Treat allergies:** Staying away from allergens and getting treatment for allergies will help to keep the immune reaction (and sniffles) under control. Never rub your eyes if they are itching. The blood vessels are quite fragile and easily damaged when we rub our eyes.

The appearance of dark circles, even those tricky hereditary ones, can be improved with the appropriate care products. With advances in treatment technology, there are options available for individuals who want to rid themselves of these gremlins. Professional treatments can range from peels and laser treatments to surgical options. For those who prefer topical treatments to treat mild to moderate dark circles, the products detailed in this chapter may be what you are looking for.

• ♥ • ♥ • ♥ • ♥ • ♥ •

Eye Contour Cream

The skin around the eyes is the most fragile area of the face. The skin in this area is incredibly thin and dehydrates quickly. This can lead to a loss in firmness and quality in circulation over time, encouraging expression lines to appear. Therefore, eye contour cream formulations must respect the skin's pH to avoid possible irritations. The formulation I'll teach you in this section is filled with active ingredients that stimulate blood circulation, improve the appearance of dark circles, increase hydration, provide water in the furrows of the skin, and inhibit the action of free radicals. Be extra careful when measuring the ingredients in the table below, keeping in mind the sensitive area the product is intended for.

Materials	Quantity 100 ml	Quantity 1 liter
Caffeine extract	1 ml	10 ml
Chamomile extract	1 ml	10 ml
Quinoa extract	1 ml	10 ml
Vitamin E	2 ml	20 ml
Base cream	10 gm	100 gm
Preservative solution	5 ml	50 ml
Cosmetic base gel	70 gm	700 gm
Distilled water	10 ml	100 ml

Directions:

In a clean, glass bowl, mix cosmetic base gel with caffeine extract, chamomile, and quinoa. Add these ingredients one at a time to the base gel and continuously stir until all of them are fully incorporated. Next, we need to hydrate the preparation by adding distilled water. Add the water a little at a time as you continue to stir. Take the gel mixture and add it to the base cream, little by little, as you keep on stirring. The goal is to create a homogenous mixture. Finally, add the vitamin E and preservative solution to your cosmetic creation. The product is now ready to be packaged and labeled. To use the cream, take a small amount and gently pat (don't rub) the product into the area around the eyes. Use smoothing movements on the eye bone from the inside out using the index finger.

· ❤ · ❤ · ❤ · ❤ · ❤ ·

Eye Contour Gel Cream

It is believed that the eye contour of a fatty face, because it contains excess lipids, does not need to be nourished. With age, the activity of the sebaceous glands increases, but in turn, there is a decrease in hydrophilic lipids that retain water, especially in the liquefied area of the eyes, so that the natural moisture of the skin is lost by evaporation. This gel cream is ideal for those with oily skin types.

Materials	Quantity 100 ml	Quantity 1 liter
Quinoa extract	2 ml	20 ml
Oat extract	2 ml	20 ml
Caffeine extract	2 ml	20 ml
Aloe vera extract	2 ml	20 ml
Vitamin E	1 ml	10 ml
Glycerin	1 ml	10 ml
Preservative solution	5 ml	50 ml
Cosmetic base gel	65 gm	650 gm
Distilled water	20 ml	200 ml
Fragrance (optional)	0,2 - 0,5 ml	2 - 5 ml

Directions:

In a clean container, carefully measure the required amount of cosmetic gel base. Add water slowly to the gel and continuously stir to hydrate the mixture. Gently stir the preservative solution in. Add the extracts one by one. Seal the container and shake well. Add vitamin E and glycerin to the mixture and mix well. At this point, you can add fragrance and coloring if desired. Measure the pH, it should have an acidity between 5.9 and 6.1. Adjust the pH if needed and package the product in a suitable container. Don't forget to indicate usage instructions and production date on the label. To use, apply the product at night after the face has been cleansed. Apply the product to the face and gently massage it in until fully absorbed.

·❤·❤·❤·❤·❤·

Strengthening Serum for Lashes and Brows

This strengthening serum nourishes and strengthens hair follicles for fuller and stronger lashes and brows. The serum is filled with nourishing ingredients that keep lashes and brows soft and easy to manage. There's no need to use preservatives in this formulation, the antioxidant properties of vitamin E will help to keep the product stable.

Materials	Quantity 100 ml	Quantity 1 liter
Castor oil	50 ml	500 ml
Almond oil	20 ml	20 ml
Vitamin E	5 ml	50 ml
Collagen	5 ml	50 ml
Biotin	10 ml	100 ml
Argan Oil	10 ml	100 ml

Directions:

In a clean glass container, mix castor, almond and argan oils. Add biotin to the oil mixture and continue to mix until the ingredient is fully incorporated. Next, we need to add vitamin E and blend it fully into the oil mixture. Lastly, add the collagen and mix to form a homogenous blend. Store in a suitable container (an applicator bottle with a brush works best) and label with the date and usage instructions. To use, lightly brush the oil on your eyebrows and lashes at night. Allow the product to work its magic throughout the night. Wash the serum off the next morning, following your usual cleansing routine.

Dark circles don't have to be a life sentence. With the right products and healthy lifestyle choices, we are able to drastically improve their appearance, resulting in a younger-looking, radiant face. It should be noted that some dark circles may need professional treatment to improve. If your dark circles are hereditary or not improving, seek the help of a skincare professional. Of course, no skincare regimen is complete without lip balm–a complimentary product that we'll learn to make in the next chapter.

·♥·♥·♥·♥·♥·

10
Complementary Products

U p until this point, we've discussed how to make various cosmetic basics. These basics are vital to any good skincare regimen. For those who are new to the world of DIY cosmetic products, it may be a bit intimidating to start creating anti-aging creams or cleansing foams right off the bat. There's no need to worry, though, if you follow the cosmetic principles highlighted at the beginning of the book your creations will turn out fine! It is always a good idea to build a bit of confidence when developing a new skill, so start by creating simple products before diving into more complex and ingredient-demanding cosmetic formulations. A good place to start building our cosmetic creation confidence is by creating lip balms. This simple and effective product is a must-have to keep chapped lips at bay and makes for an excellent product to expand your possible skincare line. In this chapter, we'll take a look at how lip balms, facial scrubs, and serums are created, and I'll share additional recommendations to keep in mind when formulating products.

· ♥ · ♥ · ♥ · ♥ · ♥ ·

Nourishing Lip Balm

There's no denying that soft, kissable lips add to our beauty, and there are plenty of reasons why we should use lip balms regularly. The skin on our lips is quite thin and prone to drying out. Anyone who has licked their lips one too many times will know just how quickly our lips can turn from soft and plump into something that resembles a scaly critter that crawled out of the Chihuahuan Desert. Lip balms are an easy and effective fix for this problem. Plus, using lip balms before applying lipstick will help to prevent that splash of color from drying out the lips in the first place. The base formulation shared in the table below can be customized with different flavors and colors and is a fun product to make.

Materials	Quantity 100 ml	Quantity 1 liter
Beeswax	20 gm	200 gm
Cocoa butter	30 gm	300 gm
Almond oil	40 ml	400 ml
Edible essence	10 gm	100 gm
Vitamin E	0.5 ml	5 ml
Oil soluble dye	S.Q. for desired	S.Q. for desired

Directions:

Using a double boiler or bain marie, melt and heat the beeswax with the cocoa butter. The melted ingredients should reach a temperature of 50 °C. Gradually, incorporate the almond oil into the melted mixture and remove it from the heat. Stir in edible essence until fully incorporated. Allow the mixture to cool to 40 °C, at this point we can add coloring and aromatize the product. Allow the product to cool and package it in a suitable container with a label.

·♥ · ♥ · ♥ · ♥ · ♥ ·

Preservative-Free Raspberry Lip Balm

This formulation is a blend of two natural waxes. Carnauba wax is an emollient which helps to soften the skin. The wax has similar properties to white beeswax, which is why these waxes can be combined (Raspberry Lip Balm, 2019). The mica in the formulation is responsible for the color. Mica is used for candle making and crafts and has a mineral origin. The pearlescent powder can be used to add color and shine to lip balms, lipsticks and other cosmetic creations. To make this sumptuous raspberry lip balm, you'll need:

Materials	Quantity 100 ml	Quantity 1 liter
Carnauba wax	10 ml	100 ml
Castor oil	77 ml	770 ml
White beeswax	8 ml	80 ml
Vitamin E	1 ml	10 ml
Raspberry essence balm	S.Q. for desired	S.Q. for desired
Ruby mica	S.Q. for desired	S.Q. for desired
Cosmetic glitter	S.Q. for desired	S.Q. for desired

Directions:

Carefully weigh the waxes and castor oil in a clean container. Melt the ingredients using a water bath. You'll need to stir constantly and be careful not to let the temperature go too high. Next, we need to add vitamin E to the mixture, followed by balm essence. Mix well so that the aroma is dispersed evenly. Pour a little bit of the melted mixture into a separate container and mix the mica in. Stir the mica and wax mixture vigorously for a few minutes to evenly disperse the color. Pour the colored mixture into the melted wax mixture when ready, and stir thoroughly to create a homogenous blend. Finally, for a touch of glamour, we can add the cosmetic glitter. Remember to stir the mixture well. The product can now be packaged and labeled.

· ♥ · ♥ · ♥ · ♥ · ♥ ·

Facial Scrub

All skin types can be exfoliated, but not all exfoliating agents are suitable for all skin types. Delicate skin will do better with scrubs making use of bamboo particles or cellulose, as these particles are very soft (*Cream Face Scrub*, 2020). For mature skin types, grape seeds, bamboo, or adzuki beans are good options. For acne-prone and oily skin, we can add a little bit of activated charcoal to the formulation to encourage a deep clean. Iberian clays are also another way we can exfoliate the skin. If you are not sure which exfoliating agent to use, it is best to opt for biodegradable wax exfoliating beads. These little particles are gentle on the skin and can be used on all skin types. Whichever exfoliating agent you use, ensure that the particles are round, otherwise, we risk giving the skin micro tears when using the product. The guidelines below detail how to create a basic scrub.

Materials	Quantity 100 ml	Quantity 1 liter
Cosmetic base gel	75 gm	750 gm
Rice extract	5 ml	50 ml
Rose extract	5 ml	50 ml
200 microns round scrub	10 ml	100 ml
Almond oil	5 ml	50 ml
Preservative solution	4 ml	40 ml
Oil soluble dye	S.Q. for desired	S.Q. for desired
Fragrance	0,2 - 0,5 ml	2 - 5 ml

Directions:

Weigh the cosmetic base gel in a container and add the two extracts. Mix the ingredients with a spatula and gently add the exfoliating particles to the mixture. Next, we need to add the preservative. Stir the mixture well and add a few drops of dye (optional). Stir the mixture for a few minutes to ensure a homogeneous blend, and package in a suitable container. Label with the date and usage instructions. To use, cleanse the face and apply the product with your fingertips to the face. Use small, circular motions to gently exfoliate the whole face. Rinse gently and complete your skincare routine.

Serum for All Skin Types

From the age of 30 onwards, the skin starts to show signs of aging. This is a time when the use of serum becomes essential. Formulated to be easily absorbed, this non-greasy, soft formulation gives the skin a long-lasting and velvety feel. As always, measure the ingredients carefully when following the instructions below.

Materials	Quantity 100 ml	Quantity 1 liter
Fragrance	1 ml	10 ml
Silicon 9040	60 ml	600 ml
Silicon 1501	10 ml	100 ml
Silicon 245	10 ml	100 ml
Isopropyl myristate	10 ml	100 ml
Vitamin E	0.5 ml	5 ml
Hyaluronic acid	10 ml	100 ml

Directions:

In a clean container, mix silicone 1501 with silicone 245. Incorporate silicone 9040 into this mixture. Set the mixture aside for a moment. In a separate container, mix fragrance with isopropyl myristate. Add vitamin E to the fragrance mixture and stir to create an even blend. Now we need to take our fragrance blend and add it to the silicone blend. Stir to form a homogenous mixture and package in a suitable container. Label with the production date and usage instructions. For easy, hygienic application, use a dropper to apply the serum to the face after cleansing and toning.

Recommendations

All formulations proposed in this material are safe for use as cosmetic products on your skin. The preservatives suggested now are the most effective to protect your creams and gels from external agents such as fungi, yeasts, and bacteria; however, I will mention in the following table alternatives of preservatives in case you decide to try other options:

Alternative preservatives	
Product	**Dose**
Benzoic acid + sodium benzoate	0,1% - 0,5%
Salicylic acid	0,1% - 0,5%
Caprylyl glycol	0,3% - 1%
Grapefruit seed extract	1% - 2%
Phenoxyethanol	0,5% - 1%
Glyceryl monolaurate	0.1% - 1%
Potassium sorbate + sodium benzoate	0,1% - 0,5%
Tocopherol (Vitamin E)	0,1 % - 1%
Carrot essential oil	1% - 2%
Rosemary extract	2% – 10%

The formulations of your products are created to obtain the proper pH levels; however, I suggest you always measure the pH of the product before packaging to ensure it is at the correct pH level. To adjust the pH level safely, keep the following in mind:

- To alkalize the product, you must use Triethanolamine.

- To acidify the product, you must use citric acid.

These components will have to be administered drop by drop until the desired pH is reached. Always remember to respect the ingredients you use. That means opting for quality ingredients, storing them safely, and measuring them accurately. When we respect our ingredients and the skin type we are formulating products for, high-quality products are born naturally.

· ♥ · ♥ · ♥ · ♥ · ♥ ·

11
Conclusion

L atina women are shown from a young age by their mothers and grandmothers that it's perfectly fine to luxuriate over themselves. We've been taught that we are worth the time and effort it takes to take care of our skin and apply our makeup perfectly. The results speak for themselves! Even if other people may see this beauty habit as indulgent, Latinas know how to take care of themselves, and they have embraced beauty wholeheartedly. It's no wonder that four of the countries that produce the most beauty pageant winners (specifically in Miss World and Miss Universe) come from Latin America! Venezuela, Brazil, and Puerto Rico have done much to keep beauty standards high in these pageants.

With so much of our culture, and by extension our identity, hinging on perfect skin, it is understandable how dark circles, acne, pigmentation stains, and wrinkles wreak havoc with our self-esteem. After all, we pride ourselves on maintaining a young and beautiful appearance. Some women may even feel naked if they leave the house without makeup on. This is not because we are vain, but because we know we are worth the effort. We love to look and feel good, and we are not afraid to splurge on quality products.

Now, I ask you: What is better than finding your favorite brand of face cream at a discount price? Making your own cosmetic products! We started this little adventure with a deep dive into the important role pH plays in skin and cosmetics, investigated how to set up a cosmetics lab at home, and delved into various cosmetic staples to formulate at home. There are many reasons why people choose to create their own cosmetic products, but I found it to be a fun and creative outlet. Creating cosmetics is both a science and an art, after all! It's a beautiful way to pay homage to our heritage and DIY-inclined nature.

Entrepreneurs who would like to dip their toes into the cosmetic industry use their creative skills to formulate innovative products. Building on the work of cosmetic chemists who use scientific methods to create stable and safe products, this book strives to provide budding entrepreneurs and skincare enthusiasts with the foundational building blocks of cosmetic science.

Formulating a product or product range always starts with an idea. Take a look at the products available in the market or conduct market research if you plan on selling your cosmetic creations. If your research determined that a new product is needed (products that are not covered in the book) it is best to seek the help of a cosmetic chemist. The chemist will help you find the right ingredients and dosages for the desired product.

Whether you are creating a new product from scratch or want to replicate the ones covered in the book, it is essential to research the raw materials needed beforehand. Some ingredients are suitable for sensitive skin, while other ingredients tend to clog pores. Researching the ingredients we intend to use thoroughly will help to ensure that harmful ingredients don't slip unintentionally into our products.

Another step we need to keep in mind is to test our products. Testing is vital to ensure that the formulation is stable and that the product performs as expected. For entrepreneurs, product testing is one of the most important steps, as it gives us precious feedback on product color, texture, viscosity, and other changeable characteristics. The goal is to create a product that is effective, looks good, and makes the user feel good—the essence of Latina beauty culture. It's a tall order, but certainly worth it!

Cosmetic science is truly a unique art. It is an art that holds the power to create living, transformative beauty. It is an art form that expresses itself on the canvass of skin, sweeping away imperfections that may nibble at our confidence. It is only natural for those who dabble in cosmetic sciences to view themselves as artists. While it is true that beauty lies in the eye of the beholder, I'll go on to argue that art lies in the hands of its creator. It is very possible for you to become that artist, and it is in this spirit that I wrote this book and shared my knowledge. The spirit of one artist sharing knowledge of the trade with another. Now that you are armed with a solid foundation, go out there and grace the world with your art!

I feel proud to write for our Latino community.

— ♥ ♥ ♥ —

If you enjoyed reading my book, please leave me your review and recommend it. Your opinion is precious to me, as it motivates me to continue researching and developing knowledge that meets our specific needs.

Hughs.
Catalina

www.artemixbeauty.com

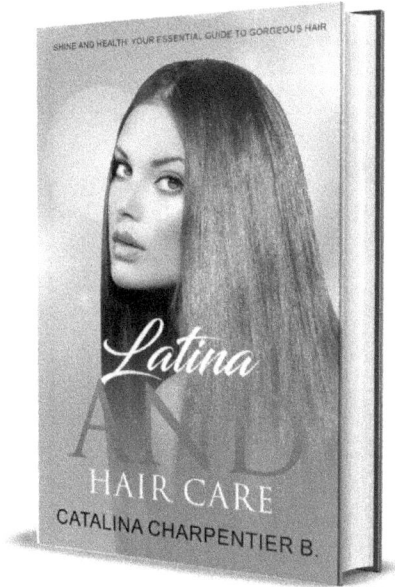

Descubre los secretos para lucir
espectacular en cada página.
Aprende sobre el cuidado de la
piel, la elección de productos y
los mejores suplementos para
rejuvenecer tu rostro.

www.artemixbeauty.com

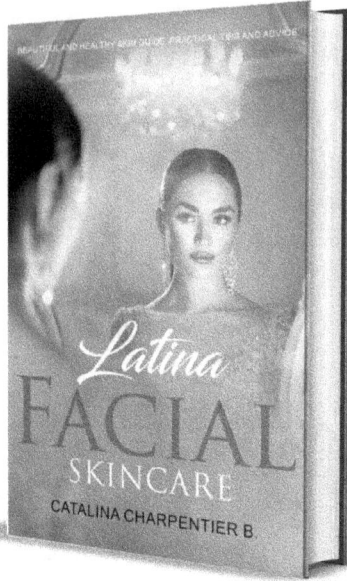

Discover the secrets to looking
spectacular on each page. Learn
about skincare, product choice,
and the best supplements to
rejuvenate your face.

www.artemixbeauty.com

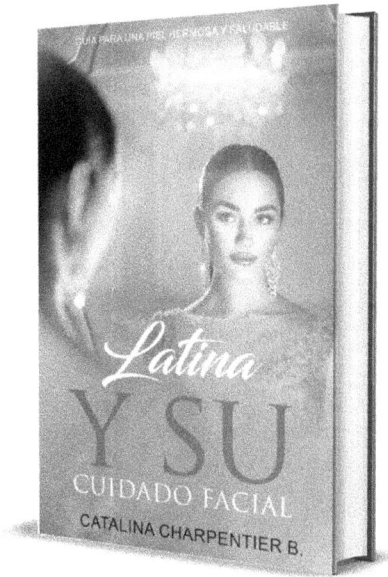

Descubre los secretos para lucir
espectacular en cada página.
Aprende sobre el cuidado de la
piel, la elección de productos y
los mejores suplementos para
rejuvenecer tu rostro.

12
Glossary

***A**dditives:* Additives are not essential to the formulation of cosmetic products, but they improve the final presentation by giving color, aroma, and protecting the product from premature deterioration.

Alkaline: A product is referred to as alkaline when it possesses a pH value between 7.1 and 14.

Alpha hydroxy acids: Water-soluble acids that gently peel away dead skin cells and aid in cell renewal. Alpha hydroxy acids are well-known for their moisturizing properties and are a popular ingredient in anti-aging products as they stimulate the production of collagen.

Anhydrous formulations: Cosmetic formulations that have little to no water content. These products are also known as "waterless" or "water-free" formulations and mainly contain oil-soluble ingredients.

Atopic dermatitis: A skin condition characterized by dry, inflamed, and itchy skin. The condition is mainly caused by irritants in personal care products, environmental factors and allergens.

Aqueous phase: The "water phase" of a cosmetic formulation. In this phase, we heat and dissolve our water-soluble ingredients. The aqueous phase is prepared separately from the oil phase.

Buffers: An ingredient used in cosmetic products to keep the pH stable.

Candelilla wax: A wax very similar to beeswax. It is derived from the Candelilla shrub that is native to Mexico. The wax acts as a humectant and is used in formulations to moisturize dry skin. Candelilla wax does not clog pores and can be safely used in formulations for oily skin types.

Caprylyl glycol: An alcohol derived from caprylyl glycol that acts as a humectant and preservative. It tends to be a safer option than most preservatives. The ingredient can be used with other preservatives to increase their antimicrobial activity.

Carnauba wax: A natural wax sometimes referred to as the "queen of waxes." Carnauba wax is the hardest natural wax available and is often used in the production of eyeliners, skin care products, and foundations.

Cetyl palmitate: A waxy emollient used in cosmetic products. The ingredient gives body and consistency to formulations.

Chelator: An ingredient used in cosmetic products to remove heavy metals.

Citric acid: An ingredient used to adjust the pH in cosmetic formulations toward an acidic value.

Coconut betaine: An ingredient with gentle cleansing properties and is often used in products designed for sensitive skin and baby products. The ingredient exerts a slight antibacterial effect.

Cocoglucoside: A mild cleansing agent derived from fruit sugar and coconut oil.

Cosmetic gel: A semi-sold product with a fresh texture. Gels are easily absorbed into the skin, and the thickness of the gel depends on how much gelling agent is used.

Crodabase CR2: A self-emulsifying base widely used in cosmetic formulations to create creams and lotions. The base is formulated with thickening waxes and emollient emulsifiers that are non-ionic, making it a skin-loving product.

Decylglucoside: A mild surfactant used in cosmetic formulations and baby products. It is non-ionic and can be used in formulations intended for individuals with sensitive skin.

Dehyquart: Also known as acetyl dimethyl ammonium chloride. It is a conditioning agent used in emulsions and creams.

Fragrance-Free: Products labeled as "fragrance-free" do not contain ingredients that are identified as cosmetic fragrance.

Hydrosols/hydrolates: These ingredients are used to partially or completely replace distilled water. Hydrosols are used to prepare toners, body gels, shampoos, and emulsions.

INCI: An abbreviation that stands for the International Nomenclature for Cosmetic Ingredients. This is an international system that is used to name cosmetic ingredients. Think of it as a common language that is used in the cosmetic industry.

Isopropyl myristate: A non-occlusive ingredient with strong emollient and spreading properties. Often used after-sun care products, facial cleansers, eye contour, and other products as it provides softness.

Microns: A unit of measurement. One micron is equivalent to a thousandth of a millimeter. It is recommended to use round particles of 200 microns for facial scrubs. Make sure the particles are round, otherwise we risk giving the skin microscopic tears.

Moisturizers: Their purpose is to help the skin retain water. Glycerin, urea, sorbitol, sodium lactate, hyaluronic acid, and betaine are commonly used moisturizing ingredients. These ingredients are best used in formulas with an aqueous phase.

Non-comedogenic: A product or ingredient that does not clog the pores. These products and ingredients are especially recommended for oily skin types.

Oil phase: The "oily phase" of a cosmetic formulation. In this phase, we heat and dissolve oil-soluble ingredients. The oil-phase is prepared separately from the aqueous phase.

Phytic acid: This ingredient is commonly used in formulations targeting acne and blackheads. It can help to shrink and clear pores. Additionally, the acid brightens the skin.

Potassium sorbate: Naturally found in some fruits, a synthetic version is made in labs for cosmetic purposes.

Rosacea: A skin condition that causes flushing, small pus-filled bumps, and visible blood vessels in the face. People with rosacea may experience periodic flare-ups.

Serum: A concentrated, liquid product designed to target specific problems such as acne, wrinkles, or uneven skin tone.

Silicone 1501: A conditioning ingredient that encourages velvety skin. The ingredient has long-lasting effects.

Silicone 245: A non-sticky ingredient with excellent spreading properties and does not leave an oily residue or buildup on the skin.

Silicone 9040: An ingredient with high molecular weight. It is compatible with numerous active ingredients and acts as a thickening agent in cosmetics formulations that are water-in-oil and water-in-silicone based.

SLS: Also known as sodium laureth sulfate. This ingredient is a surfactant that is commonly used in shampoos, floor cleaners and engine degreasers. Sodium laureth sulfate lathers well, but is harsh on the skin.

Specific action assets: These ingredients are used to enhance the action of a cosmetic. For example, Q10 can be used to add an anti-wrinkle function to skincare formulations.

Stearic acid: This ingredient acts as an emulsifier, natural thickener, and moisturizing lipid. Stearic acid may help to improve both the consistency and shelf life of an emulsion and is frequently used in cosmetic products for the face, body, and hair.

Texapon: A surfactant found in many cleaning products.

Titanium dioxide: This ingredient is commonly used as an opacifier and colorant in cosmetic ingredients.

Toner: A liquid product designed to deliver hydration to the face and to restore the skin's natural pH after cleansing.

Triethanolamine: A non-active ingredient that is used to adjust the pH of cosmetic formulations towards an alkali value.

Tween 20: Also known as polysorbate 20. This ingredient is commonly used as an emulsifying agent when preparing oil-in-water emulsions.

Unscented: Products labeled as "unscented" have no discernible scent, but may still contain cosmetic fragrance that has a neutral scent.

Xanthan Gum: A natural gelling agent used in many natural cosmetic products.

Zinc oxide: A white powder that cannot be dissolved in water, this ingredient is used in cosmetic products to treat or prevent minor skin irritation. Zinc oxide has sunscreen qualities, but should not be used as a replacement for sunscreen formulated for your skin type.

13
References

A *cidos en cosmetica: ¡descubre el mejor para tu piel!* (2020, January 17). Hacer Cremas. https://www.hacercremas.es/acidos-en-cosmetica/

Basic Concepts of Cosmetic Chemistry. (2019, May 14). MiiN Cosmetics. https://miin-cosmetics.com/blog/conceptos-basicos-quimica-cosmetica-2/

Brooks, A. (2022, August 23). *What's the Difference Between AHA vs. BHA Exfoliants?* Mira. https://www.talktomira.com/post/whats-the-difference-between-aha-vs-bha-exfoliants

Burhop Fallon, B. (2021, July 1). *Latinx Beauty Is Hotter Than Ever, and These Are the Brands on Our Radar.* NewBeauty. https://www.newbeauty.com/latinx-beauty-trend/

Cómo hacer un gel base con goma xantana. (2020, December 20). Curso de Cosmética Online. https://cursodecosmetica.com/como-hacer-un-gel-base-con-goma-xantana/

Cream Base - Uses, Side Effects, and More. (n.d.). WebMD. Retrieved November 27, 2022, from https://www.webmd.com/drugs/2/drug-8205/cream-base-topical/details

Cream face scrub. (2020, October 2). Hacer Cremas. https://www.hacer cremas.es/exfoliante-facial-en-crema/

Cremas base: qué son, cuál elijo para mi piel y recetas sencillas. (2021, July 21). Blog de Gran Velada. https://www.granvelada.com/blog/diferencias-entre-las-crema-base/#:~:t ext=Crema%20base%20hidratante&text=Es%20una%20crema%20base% 20con

Debayle, E. (2018, March 25). 9 tips para mantener el pH de la piel. *The Beauty Effect.* https://www.thebeautyeffect.com/piel/ph-de-la-piel-10-m aneras-para-mantenerlo/

EDTA. (n.d.). L'Oréal. Retrieved November 28, 2022, from https://inside-our-products.loreal.com/ingredients/edta#:~:text=i n%20the%20laboratory.-

Emulsion Mixing with Cosmetics. (n.d.). Growing Labs. https://www.gr owinglabs.com/pages/emulsion-mixing-with-cosmetics

Feregotto, T. (2019, August 3). *Requisitos de etiquetado para cosméticos comercializados en EE. UU.* CE.way. https://ceway.eu/es/requisitos-de-e tiquetado-para-cosmeticos-comercializados-en-ee-uu/

Final Report on the Safety Assessment of Trichloroethane. (2008). *International Journal of Toxicology, 27,* 107–138. https://doi.org/10.1080/10 915810802550835

Geier, J., Uter, W., Pirker, C., & Frosch, P. J. (2003). Patch testing with the irritant sodium lauryl sulfate (SLS) is useful in interpreting weak reactions to contact allergens as allergic or irritant. *Contact Dermatitis, 48*(2), 99–107. https://doi.org/10.1034/j.1600-0536.2003.480209.x

Hacer serum vitamina C. (2015, February 13). Hacer Cremas. https://w ww.hacercremas.es/hacer-serum-de-vitamina-c/

How to make homemade soap for the face. (2016, November 23). Hacer Cremas. https://www.hacercremas.es/como-hacer-jabon-dermoprotecto r-para-pieles-sensibles/

Hyaluronic acid. (2019, November 30). Wikipedia; Wikimedia Foundation. https://en.wikipedia.org/wiki/Hyaluronic_acid

Hypersensitivity   in   general.   (n.d.).   Eucerin. https://int.eucerin.com/skin-concerns/hypersensitive-redness-prone-skin /hypersensitivity-in-general#:~:text=Hypersensitive%20skin%20%2D%2 0or%20very%20sensitive

Is Benzalkonium Chloride Safe? (2022, April 18). GlanHealth. https://g lanhealth.com/blog/is-benzalkonium-chloride-safe/

Killip,   S.   (2022,   August   15).   *Beauty   &   Cosmet-ics   Market   Size: Growth   and   Industry   Trends.*   At-test. https://www.askattest.com/blog/articles/beauty-cosmetics-market -size#:~:text=In%202022%2C%20worldwide%20revenue%20from

Kunin, A. (n.d.). *Oily Skin.* DERMAdoctor Blog. https://www.dermad octor.com/blog/oily-skin-info/

La Piel y el pH - Medición, Escala y Cosméticos. (2021, January 14). Jabonarium Shop. https://www.jabonariumshop.com/la-piel-y-el-ph-m edicion-escala-y-cosmeticos-caseros

Leiva, C. (2019). *11 reasons why your skin could be oily.* Insider. https:// www.insider.com/why-is-your-skin-oily-2019-5

Lincho, J., Martins, R. C., & Gomes, J. (2021). Paraben Compounds—Part I: An Overview of Their Characteristics, Detection, and Impacts. *Applied Sciences, 11*(5), 2307. https://doi.org/10.3390/app110 52307

Nast, C. (2018, May 16). *11 Things Dermatologists Want You to Know About Sensitive Skin*. SELF. https://www.self.com/story/sensitive-skin-f acts-dermatologists

Nikolic, A. (2016, April 10). *Treating Oily Skin: Choosing The Right Ingredients*. SkinMiles. https://skinmiles.com/treating-oily-skin-choosing -right-ingredients/#:~:text=Oily%20skin%20can%20be%20hard

Photosensitivity. (2011, February 2). National Cancer Institute. https://www.cancer.gov/publications/dictionaries/cancer-terms/de f/photosensitivity

Preservatives In Skincare: What You Need To Know. (n.d.). Esmi Skin. Retrieved November 30, 2022, from https://www.esmiskin.com/blogs/esmi-skin-central/preservatives-in-skin care-what-you-need-to-know#:~:text=Some%20have%20been%20linked %20to%20serious%20long%20term%20health%20issues%20too.&text=T he%20most%20widely%20used%20preservatives

Raspberry lip balm. (2019, January 13). Hacer Cremas. https://www.ha cercremas.es/hacer-balsamo-labial-aroma-frambuesa-brillo/

Regulation (EC) No 1223/2009 of the European Parliament. (2022). Eur-Lex. https://eur-lex.europa.eu/legal-content/EN/TXT/?uri=CELE X%3A02009R1223-20221006

Ruiz, G. (2016). *La vanidad de la mujer latina, en cifras*. Univision. https://www.univision.com/estilo-de-vida/belleza/la-vanidad-de-la-mujer-latina-en-cifras

Saffari, K. (2019). *Overview of the Hispanic Travel Market*. https://ntaonline.com/wp-content/uploads/2019/10/Overview-of-the-Hispanic-Travel-Market.pdf

Steadman, K. (2017, May 18). *The Root of Oil Evil: Top 7 Causes of Oily Skin*. MYSA. https://www.foreo.com/mysa/top-7-causes-oily-skin/#:~:text=Genetics

Stern, R. (2004). Hyaluronan catabolism: a new metabolic pathway. *European Journal of Cell Biology, 83*(7), 317–325. https://doi.org/10.1078/0171-9335-00392

Texapon. (2022). Constru Químicos. https://construquimicos.com.co/materias-primas/177-texapon.html

Texapon liquido. (2021, May 1). Productos Mima. https://www.productosmima.com/texapon-liquido/

Tipos de conservantes cosméticos: ¿qué debes saber sobre ellos? (2021, June 23). ZS España. https://www.zschimmer-schwarz.es/noticias/tipos-de-conservantes-cosmeticos-que-debes-saber-sobre-ellos/

Triclosan: Health Effects. (n.d.). Beyond Pesticides. https://www.beyondpesticides.org/resources/antibacterials/triclosan/health-effects

Understanding skin – Skin's pH. (2017, April 4). Eucerin; Eucerin. https://int.eucerin.com/about-skin/basic-skin-knowledge/skins-ph

Vallez, M. (2021, April 27). *Requisitos de etiquetado de cosméticos según el Reglamento 1223/2009 de la UE - Las Normas ISO.* Las Normas Iso. https://www.lasnormasiso.com/requisitos-de-etiquetado-de-cosmet icos-segun-el-reglamento-1223-2009-de-la-ue/

Watson, K. (2020, July 27). *Veins Under Eyes: Causes and Treatment Options.* Healthline. https://www.healthline.com/health/what-causes-pr ominent-veins-beneath-the-eyes-and-how-to-treat-them

What Happens to Collagen as We Age. (2020, April 3). Vibrance MedSpa. https://vibrancemedspa.com/what-happens-to-collagen-as-we -age/#:~:text=Your%20body%20begins%20to%20lose

What Is Cosgard (Geogard 221). (n.d.). Learn Canyon. https://learncan yon.com/ingredients/cosgard/

Why Is Product Labeling So Important? (2017, October 23). Luminer. https://www.luminer.com/articles/why-is-product-labeling-important/

Williams, D. (2016, December 1). *How the Cosmetics Industry Embraced Technology.* Toppan Digital Language. https://toppandigital.com/transl ation-blog/cosmetics-industry-embraced-technology/

Image References

A. Shkraba. (2020). *Lip Balms in Can Containers.* https://www.pexels.c om/photo/lip-balms-in-can-containers-6187571/

A. Shvets. (2020). *Crop black woman making aromatic liquid in-cense.* https://www.pexels.com/photo/crop-black-woman-making-arom atic-liquid-incense-5760907/

Cottonbro. (2020). *[Person holding pot of cream]*. https://www.pexels.co m/photo/hands-woman-girl-morning-4046316/

Cottonbro. (2020). *Person Holding White Plastic Bottle*. https://www.p exels.com/photo/person-holding-white-plastic-bottle-4612151/

Cottonbro Studio. (2020). *Person Holding Silver Wire Whisk Mixing Hair Color*. https://www.pexels.com/photo/person-holding-silver-w ire-whisk-mixing-hair-color-3993315/

Cottonbro Studio. (2021). *A Woman Touching a Pump Bottle*. https://w ww.pexels.com/photo/a-woman-touching-a-pump-bottle-7449903/

J. Burrow. (2021). *Abstract background of wavy gel fluids with smooth texture*. https://www.pexels.com/photo/abstract-background-of-wavy-g el-fluids-with-smooth-texture-6402532/

K. Grabowska. (2020). *Set of cosmetic bottle with pink rose on wooden plate*. https://www.pexels.com/photo/set-of-cosmetic-bottle-with-pi nk-rose-on-wooden-plate-4041391/

K. Grabowska. (2020). *Person Holding White Plastic Bottle*. https://ww w.pexels.com/photo/person-holding-white-plastic-bottle-4938450/

Kindel Media. (2021). *A Yellow Liquid in a Beaker*. https://www.pexels. com/photo/a-yellow-liquid-in-a-beaker-8325703/

Mart Production. (2021). *Clear Glass Bottles on White Wooden Shelf*. https://www.pexels.com/photo/clear-glass-bottles-on-white-wood en-shelf-8450391/

Ольга Волковицкая. (2022). *Round Glass Jar with Black Lid*. https://w ww.pexels.com/photo/round-glass-jar-with-black-lid-10860492/

P. Kovaleva. (2021). *Close Up Photo of Containers.* https://www.pexels.co m/photo/close-up-photo-of-containers-8101531/

R. Barros. (2019). *Sitting and Laughing Woman.* https://www.pexels.co m/photo/sitting-and-laughing-woman-1996887/

R. Lach. (2021). *Woman washing her face.* https://www.pexels.com/pho to/woman-washing-her-face-8142194/

R. Lach. (2021). *Woman in lab coat using smartphone.* https://www.pex els.com/photo/woman-in-lab-coat-using-smartphone-9795013/

R. Lach. (2021). *White Labeled Clear Plastic Bottle.* https://www.pexels .com/photo/white-labeled-clear-plastic-bottle-8128069/

S. Chai. (2021). *Crop person showing bottle with liquid.* https://www.pex els.com/photo/crop-person-showing-bottle-with-liquid-7262687/

S. Chai. (2021). *Green dispensers on shelf on shower system.* https://www.p exels.com/photo/green-dispensers-on-shelf-on-shower-system-7262993/

Shvets Production. (2021). *Facial Wash on Silicone Cleansing Pad.* https://www.pexels.com/photo/facial-wash-on-silicone-cleansing -pad-9775328/

9 781961 176133